One Step at a Time
The Strategic Guide to the New Year and Beyond: Innovation, Growth, and Resilience

From the experience of Origami's team members

Collected and reviewed
by Raffaella Grassi

For Origami Group
Origami Engineering
3rd Fl., 28 Austin Friars - London EC2N 2QQ - United Kingdom

Raffaella Grassi - Origami Group

One Step at a Time

The Strategic Guide to the New Year and Beyond: Innovation, Growth, and Resilience

Published by Lulu.com

Copyright © 2024 by Raffaella Grassi

All rights reserved. No part of this book may be reproduced or transmitted by any means, electronic or mechanical, including photocopying, recording, or by any information storage or retrieval system without written permission from the author or publisher, except for inclusion of brief excerpts in reviews and articles.

ISBN 978-1-326-82795-3

New Edition

Printed and Bound in the United States of America

Cover Design: Lulu.com

Cover Design: Raffaella Grassi

Raffaella Grassi Copyright © 2024 by Raffaella Grassi

DISCLAIMER AND TERMS OF USE AGREEMENT

The author and publisher have used their best efforts in preparing this report. The author and publisher make no representation or warranties with respect to the accuracy, applicability, fitness, or completeness of the contents of this report. The information contained in this report is strictly for educational purposes. Therefore, if you wish to apply ideas contained in this report, you are taking full responsibility for your actions. EVERY EFFORT HAS BEEN MADE TO ACCURATELY REPRESENT THIS PRODUCT AND IT'S POTENTIAL. HOWEVER, THERE IS NO GUARANTEE THAT YOU WILL IMPROVE IN ANY WAY USING THE TECHNIQUES AND IDEAS IN THESE MATERIALS. EXAMPLES IN THESE MATERIALS ARE NOT TO BE INTERPRETED AS A PROMISE OR GUARANTEE OF ANYTHING. SELF-HELP AND IMPROVEMENT POTENTIAL IS ENTIRELY DEPENDENT ON THE PERSON USING OUR PRODUCT, IDEAS AND TECHNIQUES. YOUR LEVEL OF IMPROVEMENT IN ATTAINING THE RESULTS CLAIMED IN OUR MATERIALS DEPENDS ON THE TIME YOU DEVOTE TO THE PROGRAM, IDEAS AND TECHNIQUES MENTIONED, KNOWLEDGE AND VARIOUS SKILLS. SINCE THESE FACTORS DIFFER ACCORDING TO INDIVIDUALS, WE CANNOT GUARANTEE YOUR SUCCESS OR IMPROVEMENT LEVEL. NOR ARE WE RESPONSIBLE FOR ANY OF YOUR ACTIONS. MANY FACTORS WILL BE IMPORTANT IN DETERMINING YOUR ACTUAL RESULTS AND NO GUARANTEES ARE MADE THAT YOU WILL ACHIEVE RESULTS SIMILAR TO OURS OR ANYBODY ELSE'S, IN FACT NO GUARANTEES ARE MADE THAT YOU WILL ACHIEVE ANY RESULTS FROM OUR IDEAS AND TECHNIQUES IN OUR MATERIAL. The author and publisher disclaim any warranties (express or implied), merchantability, or fitness for any particular purpose. The author and publisher shall in no event be held liable to any party for any direct, indirect, punitive, special, incidental or other consequential damages arising directly or indirectly from any use of this material, which is provided "as is", and without warranties. As always, the advice of a competent professional should be sought. The author and publisher do not guarantee the performance, effectiveness or applicability of any sites listed or linked to in this report. All links are for information purposes only and are not warranted for content, accuracy or any other implied or explicit purpose. All people and events described herein are true at the best of the author's knowledge. People's names could have been changed or partly omitted for privacy reasons if name and/or information is not already available to public domain.

Raffaella Grassi - Origami Group

To my incredible team and collaborators
who inspire and support me every step of the way.
This work is a reflection of our shared vision
and dedication to making a positive impact.

One Step at a Time

Contents

Preface .... g

Introduction: Setting the Stage for a Year of Purpose-Driven Innovation 1

Overview of Origami Group's Values and the Toolkit's Purpose ... 2

Message from Origami's Leadership on the Importance of Aligning Growth with Purpose and Sustainability 5

Chapter 1: Top Innovation Trends Shaping the New Year 8

Overview of Emerging Trends and Technologies in Innovation ... 9

    Artificial Intelligence and Machine Learning (AI/ML) 9

    Quantum Computing 10

    Internet of Things (IoT) and Edge Computing 10

    Sustainable Technology 11

    5G and Next-Gen Connectivity 12

    Biotechnology and Genetic Engineering 12

    Blockchain and Decentralized Finance (DeFi) 13

How These Trends Can Impact Various Industries and Influence Strategic Growth 14

    Manufacturing and Supply Chain Management 14

    Healthcare and Pharmaceuticals 15

    Finance and Decentralized Systems 15

    Retail and Consumer Goods 15

    Agriculture and Food Production 16

Chapter 2: The Essential of Innovation Engineering 17

Introduction to the Principles of Innovation Engineering 18

Practical Examples and Case Studies Showcasing Innovative Engineering Applications in Business 21

    Healthcare: Implementing AI-Driven Diagnostics 21

    Manufacturing: Reducing Downtime with IoT and Predictive Maintenance 22

    Retail: Enhancing Customer Experience with Augmented Reality (AR) 23

Financial Services: Streamlining Compliance with Blockchain Technology 24

Chapter 3: Strategic Planning for Sustainable Growth 25

Guiding Principles for Developing a Strategic Growth Plan 26

Start with a Clear Vision 26

Prioritize Resilience and Adaptability 27

Align Short-Term Objectives with Long-Term Goals 28

Cultivate a Culture of Innovation 28

Engage Stakeholders in the Planning Process 28

Establish Measurable KPIs and Benchmarks 29

Commit to Continuous Evaluation and Improvement 29

Embrace Technology as an Enabler of Growth 30

Focus on Purpose-Driven Leadership 30

Tools and Frameworks to Align Goals with Long-Term Business Vision and Purpose 31

SWOT Analysis 31

Balanced Scorecard 32

OKR (Objectives and Key Results) 32

PESTLE Analysis 33

Scenario Planning 33

Theory of Change 34

Hoshin Kanri (Policy Deployment) 34

Design Thinking 34

Chapter 4: Leadership in the Age of Innovation 36

Key Leadership Qualities for Driving Innovation and Resilience 37

Visionary Thinking 37

Emotional Intelligence 38

Adaptability 38

Courage and Willingness to Take Risks 39

Empathy and Inclusivity 39

Focus on Continuous Learning 40

Effective Communication 40

Resilience and Perseverance 41

Strategic Thinking and Foresight 41

    Empowerment and Delegation 42

Strategies for Cultivating a Team Culture That Embraces Change and Creativity 43

    Promote Psychological Safety..43

    Encourage Collaborative Problem-Solving 44

    Provide Opportunities for Continuous Learning.. 44

    Reward Innovation and Celebrate Successes 44

    Embrace Flexible Work Structures 45

    Set Clear Goals and Provide a Vision for Change..45

    Foster a Growth Mindset 46

    Involve Team Members in Decision-Making 46

    Provide the Tools and Resources Needed for Innovation 47

    Lead by Example 47

Chapter 5: Sustainability as a Growth Strategy 49

Embedding Sustainability into Business Strategy 50

    Define a Clear Sustainability Vision and Goals 50

    Incorporate Sustainability into Core Values and Culture 51

    Assess the Entire Supply Chain 51

    Invest in Sustainable Product Design 52

    Use Data to Drive Sustainable Decision-Making 52

    Engage with Stakeholders...53

    Align Sustainability with Innovation and Growth 53

    Set Long-Term Goals and Short-Term Milestones 54

    Educate and Empower Employees 55

    Measure, Report, and Communicate Sustainability Efforts.............................55

Benefits of Sustainable Practices for Brand Reputation, Customer Loyalty, and Long-Term Profitability 56

    Enhanced Brand Reputation 56

    Building Customer Loyalty...57

    Long-Term Profitability Through Cost Savings 57

    Increased Market Share and Consumer Trust 58

    Resilience Against Market Fluctuations..58

Access to Capital and Investment Opportunities 59
Regulatory Compliance and Risk Mitigation 60
Strengthening Community and Social Impact.. 60
Innovation and Competitive Advantage 61

Chapter 6: Preparing your Organization for Innovation Readiness 62

Steps to Assess and Enhance Organizational Readiness for Innovation 63

Conduct an Innovation Readiness Assessment 63
Evaluate Leadership Commitment to Innovation.. 64
Assess Resource Availability and Allocation 64
Identify and Develop Skills for Innovation 65
Evaluate Organizational Structure and Decision-Making Processes 65
Examine the Culture of Risk-Taking and Experimentation 66
Align Innovation Goals with Business Strategy 66
Foster a Collaborative Environment 67
Establish Metrics to Measure Innovation Readiness and Success................... 67
Communicate and Reinforce the Innovation Vision 68

Tips for Ensuring that Structures, Processes, and Culture Support Growth and Adaptability 68

Adopt an Agile Organizational Structure... 69
Implement Flexible, Adaptive Processes 69
Encourage Open Communication and Knowledge Sharing.............................. 69
Provide Access to Necessary Resources and Tools 70
Incentivize and Reward Innovation Efforts 70
Empower Teams to Make Decisions 71
Establish Clear Innovation Goals and Objectives 71
Foster a Culture of Continuous Learning 71
Encourage Experimentation and Accept Failure as Learning 72
Integrate Sustainability and Social Responsibility 72

Chapter 7: Purpose-Driven Innovation Aligning Growth with Core Values 74

Purpose-Driven Innovation and Its Impact on Brand Identity 75

Understanding Purpose-Driven Innovation.. 75

The Impact of Purpose on Brand Identity 76
Building Customer Loyalty Through Purpose 77
Differentiating in a Competitive Market 78
Attracting and Retaining Top Talent 78
Creating a Lasting Legacy 79
Challenges and Considerations 79

Case Studies and Examples of Companies Leading with Purpose. 80

Patagonia: Environmental Stewardship and Ethical Business Practices 81
Unilever: Sustainable Living Plan 81
Tesla: Advancing Clean Energy Solutions 82
The Body Shop: Ethical Sourcing and Social Responsibility 83
Warby Parker: Social Impact Through Vision Accessibility 83

Chapter 8: Building a Roadmap for the New Year and Beyond ... 88

Guidance on Creating a Strategic Roadmap for the New Year ... 89

Define Your Vision and Objectives 89
Conduct a SWOT Analysis 90
Establish SMART Goals 90
Prioritize Initiatives and Milestones 91
Allocate Resources and Set a Budget 92
Assign Responsibilities and Build Accountability 92
Set Up Tracking and Reporting Mechanisms 93
Create a Timeline with Quarterly Goals 93
Plan for Flexibility and Adaptability 94
Communicate the Roadmap to the Organization 94

Practical Tools: the New Year Roadmap Template, Quarterly Goals, and Action Plans 95

the New Year Roadmap Template 95
Quarterly Goals Framework 96
Action Plan Checklist 97
Dashboard for Progress Tracking 98
Monthly Review and Adjustment Meetings 99

Chapter 9: Committing to Growth and Innovation in the New Year 100

Encouragement to Take the First Steps Toward Implementing These Insights 101

Begin with a Clear and Purpose-Driven Vision 101

Identify Immediate Priorities and Take Action 102

Empower Teams to Innovate and Contribute 102

Establish a Roadmap and Set Quarterly Goals 103

Cultivate a Culture of Learning and Adaptability 103

Focus on Sustainability as a Core Strategy 104

Leverage Data to Drive Decision-Making 104

Build and Nurture Relationships with Stakeholders 105

Commit to Continuous Reflection and Improvement 105

Take the First Step Today 106

Origami Group's Commitment to Supporting Clients on Their Journey 106

A Client-Centered Approach to Support 107

Expertise Across a Range of Industries 107

Guidance on Purpose-Driven Innovation 107

Customized Roadmap Development and Strategic Planning 108

Continuous Support and Adaptability 109

Access to Practical Tools and Resources 109

Cultivating a Culture of Innovation and Learning 110

Celebrating Success and Learning from Challenges 110

A Long-Term Partnership Committed to Your Success 110

Preface

In an age defined by rapid change and unprecedented challenges, the ability to innovate, adapt, and grow purposefully has become essential.

This book, *One Step at a Time, The Strategic Guide to the New Year and Beyond: Innovation, Growth, and Resilience*, is designed to serve as a blueprint for leaders, managers, and innovators who recognize that thriving in the modern landscape requires more than just following traditional paths.

It calls for a proactive, structured approach that balances resilience, sustainability, and growth in a way that meets the demands of an increasingly complex world.

Throughout my career in engineering, business development, and strategic consultancy, I have had the privilege of working with organizations across diverse industries and markets, all facing unique challenges and opportunities.

From energy and industrial engineering to material science and innovation in health and sustainability, I have witnessed firsthand how effective strategies can turn obstacles into catalysts for progress.

The insights in this book are drawn from years of experience, practical applications, and collaboration with professionals and innovators who have shown me the importance of purpose-driven, adaptable growth in an ever-evolving environment.

This book explores a comprehensive range of themes that are central to building a forward-looking, adaptable organization.

It begins with an overview of *Top Innovation Trends Shaping Years Ahead*, offering insights into the latest advancements in technology and their potential to redefine industries.

We then delve into the *Essentials of Innovation Engineering*, a structured approach to nurturing creativity that allows organizations to not only ideate but also implement meaningful change effectively. By integrating these practices, businesses can foster a culture of innovation that supports sustainable growth over the long term.

Following this, we address the critical need for *Strategic Planning for Sustainable Growth*. In a world where short-term gains are often prioritized, this chapter emphasizes the importance of aligning growth objectives with environmental, social, and economic sustainability.

Creating strategies that balance profit with responsibility helps organizations build trust, attract talent, and achieve resilience in a competitive market.

The role of leadership is also a core focus. In *Leadership in the Age of Innovation*, we examine the essential qualities that leaders need to drive change and inspire teams.

Effective leaders must be adaptable, emotionally intelligent, and visionary, capable of guiding their organizations through both challenges and opportunities.

This chapter provides actionable insights for cultivating a team culture that embraces creativity and change—qualities that are crucial for long-term success.

We then explore *Sustainability as a Growth Strategy*, highlighting how integrating sustainable practices into business strategies can enhance brand reputation, foster customer loyalty, and improve profitability.

With climate change, resource scarcity, and social equity at the forefront of global concerns, sustainability is no longer optional; it is a strategic imperative.

This section provides a roadmap for embedding sustainability into the core of your organization, demonstrating that businesses can achieve growth and make a positive impact simultaneously.

As the book progresses, we move toward practical applications with *Building a Roadmap for the New Year and Beyond*. This chapter offers guidance on developing a structured, actionable plan that aligns with the organization's vision and prepares it to thrive in an uncertain world.

Through templates, quarterly goals, and action plans, readers will learn how to create a roadmap that provides direction and keeps teams focused on high-impact activities.

To ensure that innovation is not only possible but also sustainable within the organization, we also examine *Preparing Your Organization for Innovation Readiness*.

This chapter covers how to assess and enhance organizational readiness, ensuring that structures, processes, and culture are equipped to support continuous growth and adaptability.

From resource allocation to risk management, this chapter provides the tools needed to build a resilient organization that can respond to evolving demands.

Finally, we conclude with *Purpose-Driven Innovation: Aligning Growth with Core Values*. While purpose-driven growth is just one aspect of the book's focus, it plays an essential role in building organizations that resonate with stakeholders on a deeper level.

This chapter underscores the power of aligning business objectives with core values, demonstrating how purpose-driven strategies can differentiate brands, enhance customer loyalty, and attract top talent.

Throughout these chapters, the book incorporates real-world case studies from companies that have successfully navigated the complexities of innovation, sustainability, and growth.

These examples showcase the strategies, challenges, and successes of organizations that are leading the way, providing readers with insights that are both practical and inspiring.

The case studies remind us that the principles discussed here are not abstract; they are applied daily by businesses that have committed to creating lasting value.

At its core, this book is about building organizations that are prepared to navigate an uncertain future with clarity, purpose, and adaptability.

My hope is that the strategies, frameworks, and tools presented here will serve as a foundation for leaders who aspire to create meaningful change.

The path to growth in today's world is not always straightforward, but by approaching innovation, sustainability, and leadership with a balanced, strategic perspective, we can create resilient organizations that thrive in the new year and beyond.

Thank you for joining me on this journey toward purposeful, sustainable growth. As you move through the chapters, I encourage you to reflect on your organization's unique strengths, values, and opportunities, and to embrace the transformative power of innovation in building a better future for all.

Introduction: Setting the Stage for a Year of Purpose-Driven Innovation

As we step into a new year, businesses face both unprecedented challenges and extraordinary opportunities.

At Origami Group, we believe that sustainable growth isn't just about innovation and adaptability; it's about aligning every decision with purpose, responsibility, and resilience.

This year, the landscape demands that organizations not only pursue excellence but also commit to making a positive, lasting impact on society and the environment.

Purpose-Driven Innovation is our guiding principle - holistic approach that combines strategic growth with a focus on sustainability, ethics, and long-term value.

This toolkit is crafted as a comprehensive guide to help you navigate the complexities of the new year with clarity and intention.

In the chapters that follow, we explore key themes like Innovation Trends, Strategic Planning, Leadership, and Organizational Readiness, each offering actionable insights and tools to align your growth strategy with core values.

The aim is not just to adapt to change but to harness it as a force for meaningful progress. Together, let's set the stage for a year where purpose-driven growth isn't just a goal, but a shared commitment to creating a better, more resilient future.

Overview of Origami Group's Values and the Toolkit's Purpose

In an era marked by rapid technological shifts, evolving consumer expectations, and pressing environmental and social challenges, businesses are called upon to redefine what success truly means.

At Origami Group, we believe that success isn't just about financial growth or market dominance; it's about building a legacy of resilience, responsibility, and purposeful action.

Our values — *Visionary Leadership*, *Strategic Innovation*, and *Sustainable Growth* — reflect our commitment to guiding organizations through these transformative times with a focus on integrity and long-term impact.

Origami Group's ethos centers around the idea that businesses today are woven into the larger fabric of society.

With every decision, there's an opportunity to positively influence not only the bottom line but also the lives of employees, communities, and the health of our planet.

Visionary leadership requires a commitment to these broader responsibilities, fostering not just growth but also trust and credibility. At Origami, we are dedicated to helping businesses step confidently into this role by equipping them with the insights, tools, and support needed to innovate responsibly.

The *Digital Toolkit* you hold in your hands is a culmination of our commitment to Purpose-Driven Innovation. This concept is fundamental to our approach and is designed to guide organizations toward meaningful progress.

Purpose-Driven Innovation means aligning business goals with a higher purpose, ensuring that each initiative reflects the values that are important to the organization and its stakeholders.

The toolkit aims to equip you with actionable strategies, practical tools, and the inspiration needed to turn these values into tangible outcomes.

In developing this toolkit, our team at Origami Group drew upon decades of experience in business consulting, innovation engineering, and sustainability practices.

Our approach is both holistic and grounded, recognizing that while each organization has its unique challenges, many of the principles of purposeful, resilient growth are universal.

We have worked across diverse sectors, witnessing firsthand the power of aligning strategy with purpose. This toolkit is a reflection of these experiences, designed to provide you with practical guidance across key areas such as *Innovation Trends, Strategic Planning, Leadership,* and *Sustainability*.

Each chapter of this toolkit is intended as a building block in your journey toward purpose-driven growth.

From understanding the latest innovation trends that are reshaping industries to strategies for embedding sustainability into your core business model, the chapters are structured to offer insights that are both forward-looking and grounded in practical application.

For example, the chapter on Strategic Planning doesn't just cover high-level frameworks; it includes step-by-step templates and checklists that help ensure each plan is actionable and aligned with long-term goals.

Likewise, the chapters on Leadership and Organizational Readiness delve into the human aspect of growth, offering tools to cultivate a culture of resilience and adaptability.

Our hope is that this toolkit will serve as more than just a guide; we want it to be a companion in your organization's journey toward sustainable, impactful growth.

As you navigate the evolving business landscape of the new year, use this toolkit as a resource to inspire, challenge, and support your decisions.

Whether you're rethinking your innovation strategy, recalibrating your organizational goals, or simply seeking new ways to engage your team, we invite you to make this toolkit your own.

Take notes, personalize the exercises, and explore how each section aligns with the unique vision you have for your business.

At Origami Group, we understand that meaningful growth requires not only a clear vision but also the courage to pursue it.

This Toolkit was designed with this journey in mind, offering a structured, adaptable approach to growth that aligns with your values and the world's evolving needs.

By committing to purpose-driven growth, you are taking a stand for a future where business serves as a force for positive change.

Thank you for choosing Origami Group as your partner in this journey, and welcome to a new year filled with possibility, purpose, and progress.

Message from Origami's Leadership on the Importance of Aligning Growth with Purpose and Sustainability

In today's interconnected world, businesses are expected to do more than simply meet quarterly targets; they are entrusted with the task of contributing to a sustainable, equitable future.

Growth for its own sake can yield short-term success, but without a purpose, it lacks the depth and resilience needed for long-term impact.

At Origami Group, we believe that aligning growth with purpose and sustainability is essential not only for building trust but also for ensuring the longevity and relevance of your business.

Growth driven by purpose is growth with intention. It considers not just the "what" but also the "why" and "how."

Purpose-driven growth doesn't mean sacrificing profitability; rather, it means enhancing it by building a foundation of trust, transparency, and positive impact.

Purpose brings clarity to decision-making, aligns teams around shared values, and creates a lasting connection with customers, partners, and communities. In this toolkit, we encourage you to consider how purpose can be embedded into every facet of your strategy, from innovation initiatives to daily operations.

Sustainability is integral to purpose-driven growth.

At Origami Group, sustainability is not an afterthought; it is embedded in our core values and in every project we undertake.

To us, sustainability is more than reducing environmental impact—it's about creating systems and practices that support social equity, economic viability, and a regenerative relationship with our planet.

By prioritizing sustainability, businesses not only protect the resources they rely on but also build resilience against market fluctuations, regulatory changes, and shifting consumer expectations.

This toolkit provides practical guidance on embedding sustainability into your growth strategy.

From sustainable innovation practices to frameworks for measuring social and environmental impact, each section is designed to help you translate your values into actionable steps.

For instance, the chapter on *Sustainable Growth* covers both high-level strategies and specific metrics that can be used to track progress over time. It also addresses the challenges that come with sustainable practices, providing insights on how to overcome them and achieve meaningful impact.

As you work through this toolkit, we encourage you to see purpose-driven growth not as a trend but as a guiding principle.

Let this toolkit inspire you to think deeply about the legacy you want your organization to leave behind. Ask yourself how your business can contribute positively to society and the environment and use the insights in each chapter to build a strategy that reflects this commitment.

Aligning growth with purpose requires a mindset shift, but it is a shift that brings fulfillment, resilience, and a deeper sense of accomplishment.

Thank you for joining us on this journey.

One Step at a Time

At Origami Group, we are here to support you as you build a future that is not only profitable but also purposeful.

This toolkit is designed to be a starting point, a resource, and a reminder of the impact that businesses can have when they lead with intention.

Together, let's create a path toward growth that is aligned with values, dedicated to sustainability, and grounded in purpose.

Chapter 1: Top Innovation Trends Shaping the New Year

Innovation is the driving force that propels businesses into the future, helping them adapt to shifting landscapes, meet evolving consumer demands, and overcome complex global challenges.

In the new year, the pace of innovation is set to accelerate as emerging technologies and evolving market needs redefine what's possible.

Staying ahead of these changes is no longer just an advantage — it's a necessity for organizations that aim to remain competitive and relevant.

This chapter explores the top innovation trends that will shape the business landscape in the coming year, from advancements in artificial intelligence and sustainable technology to breakthroughs in digital transformation and automation.

Each trend reflects not only a technological leap but also a response to the pressing challenges of our time, such as climate change, resource scarcity, and the need for resilient, adaptable business models.

By understanding these trends, leaders can make informed, strategic decisions that align with their organization's values and objectives.

The goal is not merely to keep pace but to leverage these innovations to drive meaningful growth, create value, and contribute positively to the world around us.

Overview of Emerging Trends and Technologies in Innovation

The approaching new year stands on the cusp of a new wave of transformative technologies that are reshaping industries, influencing consumer behavior, and challenging businesses to innovate like never before.

These trends are more than technological advancements — they represent profound shifts in how we approach sustainability, efficiency, and human-centered design in business.

Here, we'll examine some of the most significant emerging trends and technologies set to define the future of innovation, with insights on why they matter and how they are positioned to impact the world.

Artificial Intelligence and Machine Learning (AI/ML)

Artificial intelligence continues to lead the charge in technological innovation, with applications expanding across sectors at an unprecedented pace.

From predictive analytics in retail to AI-driven diagnostics in healthcare, machine learning models are empowering organizations to automate complex tasks, derive insights from vast data sets, and make faster, data-driven decisions.

In the new year, we're likely to see a greater emphasis on AI ethics, with businesses focusing on transparency, bias mitigation, and responsible use to address societal concerns around privacy and fairness.

Additionally, AI-driven personalization in customer experience will become a key differentiator, as organizations leverage real-time data to tailor interactions at every touchpoint.

Quantum Computing

Quantum computing is no longer a distant dream; it's becoming a tangible reality with profound implications for industries reliant on complex data processing.

Capable of solving problems beyond the reach of classical computers, quantum computing opens new frontiers in fields such as cryptography, logistics optimization, and pharmaceuticals.

As companies like IBM and Google make strides in quantum technology, businesses that are quick to understand its applications could unlock significant competitive advantages, particularly in sectors like finance, cybersecurity, and material sciences.

Internet of Things (IoT) and Edge Computing

The Internet of Things (IoT) continues to expand, with billions of devices collecting data from environments, machinery, and users.

Paired with edge computing, which processes data closer to where it is generated, IoT is creating unprecedented opportunities for real-time insights and efficiency gains.

In industries such as manufacturing and logistics, IoT-enabled sensors and edge computing platforms are facilitating predictive maintenance, improving supply chain transparency, and reducing downtime.

As the world becomes increasingly connected, IoT will play a pivotal role in creating smart cities, optimizing energy use, and enhancing public safety.

Augmented Reality (AR) and Virtual Reality (VR)

Augmented and virtual reality are transforming the ways we interact with digital content, opening new avenues for immersive customer experiences and remote collaboration.

In sectors like retail and real estate, AR allows consumers to visualize products or spaces in a highly interactive way, while VR is making remote training and onboarding more effective than ever.

As hardware becomes more accessible and user-friendly, AR and VR are set to become mainstream tools in enhancing customer engagement and streamlining workflows in fields such as healthcare, education, and construction.

Sustainable Technology

With climate change at the forefront of global concerns, sustainable technology is no longer optional — it's imperative.

Innovations in renewable energy, sustainable manufacturing practices, and circular economy models are pushing industries to reduce waste, conserve resources, and minimize carbon footprints.

Businesses are exploring sustainable alternatives, such as biodegradable materials, energy-efficient processes, and carbon capture technology, which align with consumer demands for eco-friendly products.

By integrating sustainability into their core strategies, companies can reduce environmental impact and appeal to a growing base of environmentally conscious customers.

5G and Next-Gen Connectivity

5G technology is redefining what's possible in terms of connectivity, enabling faster data transfer speeds, reduced latency, and a massive increase in connected devices.

For industries like autonomous driving, healthcare, and smart cities, 5G opens up new possibilities for innovation.

Telemedicine, for example, becomes more feasible with 5G's low latency, while autonomous vehicles rely on rapid data processing to function safely.

As businesses adopt 5G infrastructure, the world will experience a new level of connectivity, allowing organizations to implement more complex IoT systems and deliver seamless user experiences across digital platforms.

Biotechnology and Genetic Engineering

Biotechnology is making leaps in areas such as genetic engineering, personalized medicine, and agricultural innovation.

With technologies like CRISPR revolutionizing the ability to edit genes, biotech holds the potential to transform healthcare by enabling targeted therapies and preventive treatments.

In agriculture, genetically engineered crops promise to improve food security and reduce pesticide use.

As ethical and regulatory frameworks evolve, biotech companies are working closely with governments and stakeholders to ensure

As the world becomes increasingly connected, IoT will play a pivotal role in creating smart cities, optimizing energy use, and enhancing public safety.

Augmented Reality (AR) and Virtual Reality (VR)

Augmented and virtual reality are transforming the ways we interact with digital content, opening new avenues for immersive customer experiences and remote collaboration.

In sectors like retail and real estate, AR allows consumers to visualize products or spaces in a highly interactive way, while VR is making remote training and onboarding more effective than ever.

As hardware becomes more accessible and user-friendly, AR and VR are set to become mainstream tools in enhancing customer engagement and streamlining workflows in fields such as healthcare, education, and construction.

Sustainable Technology

With climate change at the forefront of global concerns, sustainable technology is no longer optional — it's imperative.

Innovations in renewable energy, sustainable manufacturing practices, and circular economy models are pushing industries to reduce waste, conserve resources, and minimize carbon footprints.

Businesses are exploring sustainable alternatives, such as biodegradable materials, energy-efficient processes, and carbon capture technology, which align with consumer demands for eco-friendly products.

By integrating sustainability into their core strategies, companies can reduce environmental impact and appeal to a growing base of environmentally conscious customers.

5G and Next-Gen Connectivity

5G technology is redefining what's possible in terms of connectivity, enabling faster data transfer speeds, reduced latency, and a massive increase in connected devices.

For industries like autonomous driving, healthcare, and smart cities, 5G opens up new possibilities for innovation.

Telemedicine, for example, becomes more feasible with 5G's low latency, while autonomous vehicles rely on rapid data processing to function safely.

As businesses adopt 5G infrastructure, the world will experience a new level of connectivity, allowing organizations to implement more complex IoT systems and deliver seamless user experiences across digital platforms.

Biotechnology and Genetic Engineering

Biotechnology is making leaps in areas such as genetic engineering, personalized medicine, and agricultural innovation.

With technologies like CRISPR revolutionizing the ability to edit genes, biotech holds the potential to transform healthcare by enabling targeted therapies and preventive treatments.

In agriculture, genetically engineered crops promise to improve food security and reduce pesticide use.

As ethical and regulatory frameworks evolve, biotech companies are working closely with governments and stakeholders to ensure safe, responsible applications, paving the way for advancements that could reshape entire industries.

Blockchain and Decentralized Finance (DeFi)

Blockchain technology is evolving beyond cryptocurrency, with decentralized finance (DeFi) emerging as a promising application in the financial sector.

DeFi offers a way to create financial systems without traditional intermediaries, which has implications for global finance, particularly in underbanked regions.

Additionally, blockchain's secure, transparent ledger system is being used in supply chain management, allowing businesses to track and verify the authenticity of products.

As blockchain becomes more integrated into business models, its potential to create transparent, efficient, and decentralized systems is being realized in various industries.

These trends represent not only advancements in technology but also shifts in how businesses operate, engage with customers, and create value.

By understanding and embracing these trends, organizations can develop strategies that are not only innovative but also resilient and adaptive to future challenges.

How These Trends Can Impact Various Industries and Influence Strategic Growth

The emerging trends discussed above are not confined to single industries; their potential to disrupt and redefine spans sectors, reshaping everything from manufacturing to healthcare to finance.

By examining how each trend influences different industries, we can better understand the strategic growth opportunities they create, as well as the potential challenges and adjustments required to stay competitive.

Manufacturing and Supply Chain Management

In manufacturing, AI-driven automation and IoT sensors are revolutionizing the factory floor.

Predictive maintenance, enabled by real-time data from IoT sensors, minimizes downtime and improves productivity, while AI algorithms optimize production processes for quality and efficiency.

Meanwhile, blockchain technology offers supply chain transparency, allowing companies to verify the authenticity of materials and track goods through each stage.

For manufacturers, integrating these technologies can reduce operational costs, improve efficiency, and enhance product quality — all essential for sustaining growth in a competitive market.

Healthcare and Pharmaceuticals

In healthcare, AI, AR/VR, and biotechnology are leading the charge toward personalized, data-driven treatments.

AI enables rapid analysis of medical data, assisting in diagnostics and predicting patient outcomes, while VR is transforming patient rehabilitation and remote surgery training.

Biotech breakthroughs like CRISPR allow for precision medicine, tailoring treatments to individual genetic profiles.

As these innovations advance, healthcare providers are positioned to offer more effective, tailored patient care, paving the way for improved health outcomes and streamlined operations.

Finance and Decentralized Systems

The financial industry is being reshaped by blockchain, DeFi, and AI. Blockchain and DeFi are creating decentralized platforms for transactions, reducing the need for intermediaries and expanding financial access to underbanked populations.

AI enhances fraud detection and customer service with predictive models and chatbots, creating efficiencies in transaction processing and customer interactions.

As financial institutions adopt these technologies, they unlock growth opportunities by expanding their services and improving customer satisfaction through automation and security.

Retail and Consumer Goods

In retail, AI and AR are enhancing the customer experience by personalizing interactions and creating immersive shopping experiences.

AI-driven recommendation engines tailor product suggestions, increasing conversion rates, while AR lets customers visualize products before purchasing. IoT provides real-time inventory tracking, ensuring stock levels are optimized.

These innovations allow retailers to increase sales, reduce costs, and foster deeper customer engagement.

Agriculture and Food Production

Biotechnology and IoT are transforming agriculture by improving yield and sustainability.

Precision farming with IoT sensors allows for efficient resource use, while genetic engineering creates crops that are more resilient to climate change.

These technologies support food security and sustainable practices, aligning agricultural businesses with environmental goals while fostering growth through increased efficiency and yield.

Each of these applications illustrates how innovation trends influence strategic growth by optimizing processes, enhancing customer experiences, and opening new revenue streams across industries.

By staying at the forefront of these technologies, businesses can position themselves for resilient, impactful growth in the new year and beyond.

Chapter 2: The Essential of Innovation Engineering

Innovation Engineering is the disciplined approach to transforming ideas into solutions that address real-world challenges, blending creativity with structured methodologies to drive continuous improvement.

As technology and market demands evolve, the ability to innovate systematically is critical for organizations looking to stay competitive, adaptable, and resilient.

Unlike traditional R&D, Innovation Engineering doesn't rely solely on breakthroughs; it emphasizes a consistent, repeatable process that fosters innovation at every level of the organization.

In this chapter, we delve into the core principles of Innovation Engineering, covering the frameworks and tools that empower teams to take concepts from idea to implementation effectively.

Through these structured approaches, businesses can reduce the risks and uncertainties associated with innovation, ensuring that resources are directed toward solutions with tangible value.

Whether you're a seasoned engineer, a project manager, or a leader seeking to embed innovation into your organization's culture, this chapter will provide foundational insights.

By understanding and applying these principles, you can turn innovation into a strategic asset, enabling your organization to respond to challenges with agility and drive sustainable growth.

Introduction to the Principles of Innovation Engineering

Innovation Engineering is a dynamic, structured approach to developing ideas and transforming them into tangible, impactful solutions.

Rooted in scientific principles, Innovation Engineering combines creativity with structured methodologies that make the innovation process more predictable and repeatable.

This process enables companies to systematize innovation across teams and functions, fostering a culture of continuous improvement and adaptability.

At its core, Innovation Engineering is about solving real-world problems through novel solutions that create value for both businesses and their customers.

The first principle of Innovation Engineering is *problem definition*. Before beginning any innovation journey, it's essential to clearly understand the problem you're trying to solve.

This requires deep empathy for customers, stakeholders, and end-users, as well as a comprehensive understanding of the market landscape.

By defining the problem accurately, organizations can direct their resources and efforts toward solutions that address real needs, rather than simply creating new products or services that may lack relevance.

Tools such as *customer journey mapping*, *root cause analysis*, and *persona development* are often used to gain insight into the problem space, allowing teams to define challenges from multiple perspectives.

The second principle, *idea generation*, is where creativity and diversity of thought come into play.

Innovation Engineering encourages cross-functional collaboration, as diverse perspectives can lead to unique, out-of-the-box ideas.

Structured brainstorming sessions, ideation workshops, and techniques such as *mind mapping*, *SCAMPER*, and *the six thinking hats* help teams generate a wide array of potential solutions.

By encouraging an environment of open exploration, Innovation Engineering aims to expand the possible solution space, allowing organizations to consider a range of ideas before narrowing down to the most viable options.

Prototyping and experimentation are critical steps in the Innovation Engineering process, enabling teams to test ideas in a controlled, low-risk environment.

Prototypes can be as simple as sketches or mock-ups, or as complex as functional models, depending on the nature of the solution being tested.

This phase is essential for understanding how an idea will function in practice and for identifying any potential flaws or limitations early on.

Rapid prototyping, iterative testing, and user feedback cycles help refine ideas before significant resources are invested, reducing the risk of failure and improving the likelihood of a successful outcome.

Once a prototype is validated, the next principle is *implementation planning*.

In Innovation Engineering, implementation is not a one-size-fits-all process. Different ideas require tailored approaches to bring them to life, from resource allocation to project timelines and stakeholder engagement.

Implementation planning includes *developing a roadmap* with specific milestones, timelines, and KPIs that guide the team in executing the solution efficiently.

Additionally, risk assessment and contingency planning are integral to this phase, ensuring that potential obstacles are anticipated and that the project remains adaptable to changes in the market or organization.

The final principle of Innovation Engineering is *measurement and continuous improvement*.

Innovation is not a static process; it requires ongoing assessment to ensure that the implemented solution meets its intended objectives and delivers value.

After a solution is launched, it's essential to track performance metrics, gather user feedback, and analyze results.

Techniques like *Lean Six Sigma* or *Total Quality Management* (TQM) can be applied to monitor and enhance performance, facilitating continuous improvement over time. By analyzing data and learning from outcomes, organizations can build on each innovation effort, applying insights to future projects.

At Origami Group, we believe that Innovation Engineering is not just for product development teams — it's a mindset that should permeate every level of the organization.

When these principles are embraced across departments, from marketing to operations to customer service, innovation becomes a shared goal that drives growth and resilience.

By embedding these principles into daily practices, organizations can turn innovation into a core competency, one that enables them to respond to challenges with agility, seize opportunities with confidence, and sustain competitive advantage over the long term.

Practical Examples and Case Studies Showcasing Innovative Engineering Applications in Business

The principles of Innovation Engineering are powerful when applied to real-world scenarios, where structured approaches transform ideas into solutions that deliver measurable results.

Below are several case studies and examples from different industries that illustrate how businesses have effectively employed Innovation Engineering to address challenges, improve processes, and drive growth.

Healthcare: Implementing AI-Driven Diagnostics

In the healthcare industry, rapid and accurate diagnostics are essential for effective patient care.

One hospital network faced challenges with diagnosing certain complex conditions, resulting in extended patient wait times and increased operational costs.

Applying the principles of Innovation Engineering, the hospital set out to create a solution that would streamline diagnostics.

The team began with thorough *problem definition*, identifying inefficiencies in data analysis and bottlenecks in the diagnostic process.

Using AI and machine learning, they developed an algorithm that could analyze patient data faster and with greater accuracy than traditional methods.

Through *prototyping and experimentation*, the algorithm was tested with historical patient data to assess its effectiveness.

Following a successful trial phase, the team moved to *implementation*, integrating the AI tool into the hospital's electronic health record system.

Regular *measurement and continuous improvement* ensured the tool remained effective, with updates based on patient feedback and ongoing research.

This innovation not only improved patient outcomes but also reduced costs and enhanced operational efficiency, demonstrating how Innovation Engineering can revolutionize healthcare delivery.

Manufacturing: Reducing Downtime with IoT and Predictive Maintenance

A global manufacturing firm was experiencing costly equipment breakdowns that disrupted production schedules and impacted profitability. To address this, the company applied Innovation Engineering principles to develop a predictive maintenance system using IoT sensors.

Beginning with a clear *problem definition*, the team identified the need to reduce unplanned downtime by predicting equipment failures before they occurred.

They implemented IoT sensors on critical machinery, which collected real-time data on temperature, vibration, and other performance indicators.

Through *experimentation*, they tested different algorithms to analyze the data, ultimately creating a model that could detect patterns indicative of potential failures.

With the predictive maintenance system in place, the firm significantly reduced downtime and saved costs associated with emergency repairs.

This example illustrates how Innovation Engineering can drive operational efficiency and resilience in manufacturing through technology and data-driven solutions.

Retail: Enhancing Customer Experience with Augmented Reality (AR)

A leading furniture retailer faced challenges in helping customers visualize products in their own spaces, often resulting in lower sales conversions. Applying the principles of Innovation Engineering, the retailer explored how AR could bridge this gap.

Starting with *problem definition*, the team identified the need for a tool that would allow customers to "place" virtual furniture in their homes before making a purchase decision.

Through *prototyping*, they developed an AR application that customers could use on their smartphones, allowing them to see how products would look in their spaces.

After a period of *experimentation* and user testing, the app was refined and launched. The AR application not only enhanced customer engagement but also increased sales conversion rates, providing a competitive edge in a crowded market.

This case highlights how Innovation Engineering can create immersive, value-driven experiences that resonate with customers and drive business growth.

Financial Services: Streamlining Compliance with Blockchain Technology

Compliance is a significant challenge in the financial industry, requiring accurate record-keeping and transparency. A financial institution turned to blockchain technology to create a more efficient, secure system for managing compliance data.

Using Innovation Engineering, the team defined the problem as a need for a reliable, transparent system that would reduce the time and cost associated with regulatory audits.

They developed a blockchain-based ledger to track transactions in real-time, creating an immutable record that simplified compliance checks.

Through *implementation planning*, the ledger was integrated into the institution's existing IT infrastructure, allowing for seamless use across departments.

This system reduced audit time, cut compliance costs, and increased data security, showcasing how Innovation Engineering can address regulatory challenges with advanced technology solutions.

Each of these examples demonstrates the versatility and power of Innovation Engineering across industries. By following a structured process, organizations can transform challenges into opportunities, creating solutions that enhance efficiency, customer satisfaction, and competitive advantage.

Chapter 3: Strategic Planning for Sustainable Growth

Strategic planning is more than just setting targets; it's a structured approach to defining a clear path for sustainable growth and long-term impact.

In today's competitive landscape, businesses are challenged to not only achieve financial success but also to align their strategies with broader goals, such as environmental sustainability, social responsibility, and innovation.

A well-crafted strategic plan acts as a roadmap, guiding organizations through changing market conditions, helping them adapt to new trends, and ensuring that growth initiatives are resilient and purposeful.

This chapter delves into the essential principles of developing a strategic growth plan, offering insights into how organizations can foster growth that is not only profitable but also sustainable and value-driven.

From defining a vision that resonates with stakeholders to aligning short-term objectives with long-term goals, we'll explore the frameworks and tools needed to develop a cohesive strategy.

Whether you're leading a startup or an established enterprise, these guidelines will equip you with actionable approaches to create a strategy that drives meaningful growth, respects environmental and social impacts, and reinforces your organization's mission.

Guiding Principles for Developing a Strategic Growth Plan

Developing a strategic growth plan involves more than identifying new markets or increasing revenue — it's about setting a vision that defines how an organization will evolve, adapt, and deliver value over time.

At its core, a strategic growth plan must be grounded in principles that ensure resilience, adaptability, and alignment with the organization's mission and values.

Here, we outline essential guiding principles to help leaders craft a strategic growth plan that balances ambition with sustainability, ensuring long-term success.

Start with a Clear Vision

A compelling vision is the foundation of any effective growth strategy. This vision goes beyond financial targets, articulating the broader impact the organization aims to achieve.

A well-defined vision guides decision-making, inspires employees, and helps stakeholders understand the organization's long-term goals.

To create a vision that resonates, leaders should ask fundamental questions: What role do we want to play in our industry? How can we make a positive impact on society and the environment?

A clear, purpose-driven vision serves as a beacon for all strategic initiatives, ensuring that growth efforts align with the organization's ultimate aspirations.

Embed Sustainability into Core Strategy

In today's business environment, sustainable practices are no longer optional — they're integral to long-term success.

Incorporating sustainability into the growth plan means recognizing and mitigating the environmental, social, and economic impacts of business activities.

This can involve implementing eco-friendly practices, supporting fair labor policies, or contributing to community welfare.

By embedding sustainability into strategic planning, organizations not only reduce risks associated with regulatory changes and resource scarcity but also enhance their brand reputation and appeal to socially conscious consumers.

Prioritize Resilience and Adaptability

A growth plan must be adaptable to remain effective in a changing world.

Market dynamics, consumer preferences, and technological advancements are constantly evolving, and businesses that can pivot quickly are better positioned for long-term success.

Building resilience into a growth strategy involves anticipating potential challenges, preparing contingency plans, and fostering a culture of flexibility.

Organizations that prioritize adaptability are better equipped to respond to disruptions, whether they stem from economic downturns, shifts in consumer behavior, or emerging competitors.

Align Short-Term Objectives with Long-Term Goals

Strategic growth planning requires a balance between short-term wins and long-term goals. Short-term objectives are essential for maintaining momentum and securing quick results, but they should always be aligned with broader, long-term ambitions.

By ensuring that short-term actions contribute to overarching goals, organizations avoid the pitfalls of reactive or fragmented decision-making.

This alignment helps maintain focus, keeps the team motivated, and reinforces the organization's commitment to its vision, ensuring that every effort contributes meaningfully to sustainable growth.

Cultivate a Culture of Innovation

Innovation is the lifeblood of sustainable growth.

A growth plan should encourage experimentation, creativity, and continuous improvement.

Cultivating a culture of innovation involves empowering employees to explore new ideas, providing resources for research and development, and rewarding innovation.

When innovation is a core value, the organization becomes more agile and better prepared to seize new opportunities, meet changing customer demands, and stay ahead of competitors.

Engage Stakeholders in the Planning Process

Sustainable growth is not achieved in isolation; it requires buy-in from various stakeholders, including employees, customers, investors, and community members.

Engaging stakeholders in the planning process ensures that the growth strategy reflects diverse perspectives and meets the needs of those affected by the organization's actions.

Stakeholder engagement also builds trust, strengthens relationships, and fosters a sense of shared purpose, making it easier to implement strategic initiatives and secure support for long-term goals.

Establish Measurable KPIs and Benchmarks

A strategic growth plan should include clear, measurable Key Performance Indicators (KPIs) that provide a tangible way to track progress.

These benchmarks enable leaders to evaluate the effectiveness of their growth initiatives, make data-driven adjustments, and communicate results to stakeholders.

KPIs should be aligned with both short-term and long-term goals, covering various aspects of the business, from financial performance and market expansion to employee satisfaction and environmental impact.

Commit to Continuous Evaluation and Improvement

The business landscape is ever-changing, and a growth plan must evolve in response. Regular evaluation is essential to ensure that the strategy remains relevant and effective.

By periodically assessing outcomes, gathering feedback, and identifying areas for improvement, organizations can refine their approach and adapt to new circumstances.

Continuous evaluation fosters a mindset of learning and improvement, enabling leaders to make timely adjustments that keep the growth strategy aligned with current trends and challenges.

Embrace Technology as an Enabler of Growth

Technology is a powerful tool that can accelerate growth, enhance efficiency, and improve decision-making.

Integrating technology into the growth plan allows organizations to leverage data, automate processes, and expand their reach.

From data analytics and AI-driven insights to digital marketing and remote collaboration tools, technology can help streamline operations and create new opportunities for growth.

By embracing technology, organizations can optimize their resources, engage customers more effectively, and build a competitive edge.

Focus on Purpose-Driven Leadership

Leadership plays a critical role in driving sustainable growth. Purpose-driven leaders inspire teams, communicate a clear vision, and demonstrate a commitment to values that resonate with employees and stakeholders alike.

In a purpose-driven organization, leaders set the tone for a culture that prioritizes ethical behavior, social responsibility, and long-term impact.

This approach not only attracts talent and enhances employee satisfaction but also builds a brand reputation that appeals to customers, investors, and partners who value integrity and purpose.

These guiding principles provide a framework for developing a strategic growth plan that is not only ambitious but also sustainable, resilient, and aligned with an organization's core values.

By incorporating these principles into the planning process, leaders can create a strategy that adapts to a dynamic environment, fosters stakeholder trust, and ensures that growth is both purposeful and enduring.

Tools and Frameworks to Align Goals with Long-Term Business Vision and Purpose

Achieving sustainable growth requires more than vision; it demands tools and frameworks that can translate that vision into concrete goals, strategies, and actions.

Below, we explore several tools and frameworks that provide structure to strategic planning, ensuring alignment between immediate objectives and the organization's overarching vision and purpose.

SWOT Analysis

SWOT (Strengths, Weaknesses, Opportunities, Threats) analysis is a foundational tool in strategic planning, offering a structured approach to assess internal and external factors affecting an organization.

By identifying strengths and weaknesses, organizations can leverage their core competencies while addressing areas for improvement.

Analyzing opportunities and threats reveals potential market openings and challenges, helping leaders develop strategies that capitalize on favorable conditions and mitigate risks.

SWOT analysis is particularly valuable in aligning short-term goals with long-term vision by highlighting factors that influence sustainable growth.

Balanced Scorecard

The Balanced Scorecard framework translates strategic objectives into measurable performance indicators across four perspectives: *financial, customer, internal processes,* and *learning and growth.*

This approach provides a balanced view of organizational performance, ensuring that growth initiatives address diverse aspects of the business.

By setting specific metrics and tracking progress across these dimensions, organizations can align their short-term objectives with the long-term vision, ensuring that all areas contribute to sustainable growth.

OKR (Objectives and Key Results)

OKRs help organizations set ambitious, measurable objectives and define the key results needed to achieve them.

This framework promotes alignment across teams by clarifying how each individual's contributions support broader goals.

OKRs encourage accountability, transparency, and focus, as teams have clear targets and regularly review progress.

By establishing OKRs that align with the organization's purpose and vision, leaders ensure that every effort contributes meaningfully to long-term goals.

PESTLE Analysis

PESTLE (Political, Economic, Social, Technological, Legal, Environmental) analysis is a framework for understanding the external factors that may impact an organization's strategy.

By examining trends and forces in each area, leaders can anticipate potential challenges and adapt their growth plans accordingly.

For example, shifts in environmental regulations may affect sustainability initiatives, while advancements in technology could open new opportunities for innovation.

PESTLE analysis helps organizations stay responsive to external influences, aligning their strategies with both current and future realities.

Scenario Planning

Scenario planning is a strategic tool that enables organizations to prepare for various future possibilities by exploring different scenarios.

By envisioning multiple outcomes, from best-case to worst-case scenarios, leaders can develop strategies that are resilient to uncertainty.

Scenario planning helps align goals with the long-term vision by fostering adaptability, ensuring that the organization is prepared to pivot as needed while staying true to its core mission and values.

Theory of Change

The Theory of Change framework is a method for linking long-term goals to specific actions by mapping out the steps required to achieve desired outcomes.

This approach involves defining the change an organization wants to create, identifying key activities, and establishing metrics for success.

The Theory of Change is particularly valuable for purpose-driven organizations, as it provides a roadmap for achieving impact in a measurable, strategic way.

By aligning daily actions with the organization's broader purpose, leaders can create a coherent strategy that supports both growth and social responsibility.

Hoshin Kanri (Policy Deployment)

Hoshin Kanri, or policy deployment, is a Japanese management framework that aligns strategic objectives with day-to-day operations. This method involves cascading goals from senior leadership down to individual departments and employees, ensuring alignment at every level of the organization.

Hoshin Kanri provides a structured approach to translating long-term vision into actionable steps, fostering a culture of continuous improvement and accountability.

Design Thinking

Design Thinking is a human-centered approach to problem-solving that emphasizes empathy, experimentation, and iteration.

By focusing on user needs and involving stakeholders in the design process, organizations can develop solutions that are both innovative and aligned with customer expectations.

Design Thinking is valuable in aligning strategic goals with long-term vision by ensuring that growth initiatives address real user needs, enhance customer satisfaction, and build loyalty.

Value Chain Analysis

Value Chain Analysis is a framework for evaluating each stage of an organization's operations to identify areas for improvement.

By examining activities from procurement to distribution, leaders can optimize processes to increase efficiency, reduce costs, and enhance value for customers.

This tool is instrumental in aligning operational goals with the organization's mission, as it helps organizations deliver quality products and services in a way that reflects their commitment to sustainability and excellence.

SMART Goals

SMART (Specific, Measurable, Achievable, Relevant, Time-bound) goals provide a straightforward structure for setting objectives that align with the organization's vision and purpose.

By defining clear, actionable targets, SMART goals help teams focus on priorities, track progress, and maintain alignment with strategic initiatives.

When applied to long-term planning, SMART goals ensure that each step supports the organization's mission, fostering a culture of accountability and continuous improvement.

Chapter 4: Leadership in the Age of Innovation

In today's rapidly evolving business landscape, the role of leadership has become more pivotal than ever.

To drive meaningful innovation and foster resilience, leaders must go beyond traditional management; they must inspire, adapt, and cultivate a forward-thinking mindset within their teams.

The Age of Innovation demands a new approach to leadership — one that embraces continuous learning, values creativity, and builds a culture of adaptability in the face of uncertainty.

This chapter delves into the essential qualities and strategies that define effective leadership in a time of constant change.

From empathy and vision to risk-taking and agility, the qualities that fuel innovation are multifaceted and dynamic. We'll explore how leaders can harness these qualities to not only navigate challenges but also turn them into opportunities for growth.

Furthermore, the chapter will discuss strategies for fostering a team culture that embraces change and creativity, ensuring that every member feels empowered to contribute to the organization's mission.

Whether you're an experienced executive or a new manager, these insights offer practical tools to help you lead with resilience and purpose in a world where change is the only constant.

Key Leadership Qualities for Driving Innovation and Resilience

In a world of continuous change, innovation is not just a choice; it's a necessity for organizations aiming to remain competitive and relevant.

To drive innovation and resilience, leaders must embody qualities that go beyond traditional leadership skills.

Today's leaders are expected to inspire creativity, foster agility, and navigate uncertainty with confidence and integrity.

Below are the key leadership qualities essential for driving innovation and building a resilient organization.

Visionary Thinking

At the heart of every innovative organization is a leader with a clear and compelling vision.

Visionary leaders are able to look beyond the immediate challenges and see the bigger picture, setting a course that aligns with the organization's values and long-term goals.

This quality is crucial in the Age of Innovation because it provides teams with a sense of direction and purpose. A visionary leader inspires others by articulating not only where the organization is going but also why it matters.

By anchoring their leadership in purpose and vision, leaders create a strong foundation for innovative thinking and resilience.

Emotional Intelligence

Emotional intelligence (EQ) is a fundamental quality for leaders who wish to inspire and connect with their teams.

Leaders with high EQ are empathetic, self-aware, and skilled at managing interpersonal relationships. They understand the impact of their words and actions on others and are able to navigate conflicts and challenges with sensitivity.

In times of innovation, EQ becomes even more important as teams may face high levels of stress and uncertainty.

A leader with strong EQ can provide support, foster trust, and create a work environment where team members feel valued and heard.

Adaptability

Adaptability is a core trait for leaders in a rapidly changing world.

Innovation often requires leaders to step outside of their comfort zones, embrace new ideas, and be willing to pivot when necessary.

Adaptive leaders are open to feedback, flexible in their approaches, and able to make quick decisions based on changing circumstances.

By demonstrating adaptability, leaders model the behavior they wish to see in their teams, encouraging a culture of resilience and agility.

In an environment where change is constant, adaptability becomes essential for seizing opportunities and staying relevant.

Courage and Willingness to Take Risks

Innovation requires courage — the courage to try new things, take risks, and accept that failure is a possible outcome. Leaders who are willing to take calculated risks create an environment where creativity and experimentation are encouraged.

This quality is particularly valuable in organizations that wish to break new ground, as it empowers teams to explore ideas without fear of judgment.

Courageous leaders are not reckless; they assess risks carefully and make informed decisions. By embracing risk as part of the innovation process, leaders foster a mindset that is open to learning and discovery.

Empathy and Inclusivity

In today's diverse work environments, inclusivity is more important than ever. Empathetic and inclusive leaders recognize the value of different perspectives and actively create spaces where all voices are heard.

By fostering a culture of inclusivity, leaders encourage diverse ideas, which is essential for innovation.

Empathy enables leaders to understand the needs and motivations of their team members, creating a supportive environment where individuals feel comfortable sharing ideas and collaborating.

Inclusivity in leadership ensures that innovation is not limited to a select few but is a collective endeavor that benefits from the full range of talents and viewpoints.

Focus on Continuous Learning

The most innovative leaders are lifelong learners who stay curious and open to new knowledge.

In a rapidly evolving world, continuous learning is essential for staying up-to-date with emerging trends and technologies.

Leaders who prioritize learning inspire their teams to do the same, creating a culture where growth and development are valued.

This quality is particularly important in industries where technological advancements and market changes are frequent. A leader who embraces learning demonstrates that innovation is a journey, one that requires ongoing effort, curiosity, and adaptability.

Effective Communication

Communication is the bridge that connects vision with action.

Leaders who communicate effectively can clearly convey their ideas, goals, and expectations to their teams, ensuring that everyone understands the direction and purpose behind innovation initiatives.

Effective communication involves not only speaking clearly but also listening actively.

Leaders who listen to their team members foster trust and collaboration, creating an environment where individuals feel safe to share their thoughts and ideas.

In the Age of Innovation, where change can bring uncertainty, transparent communication is essential for maintaining alignment and building a cohesive team.

Resilience and Perseverance

Resilience is the ability to bounce back from setbacks and continue moving forward, even in the face of adversity.

Innovative leaders understand that failure is part of the journey and use challenges as opportunities for growth.

Resilience allows leaders to navigate difficulties without losing sight of their goals, maintaining momentum even when the path is uncertain.

This quality is particularly important in the innovation process, where not every idea will succeed, but every experience can provide valuable lessons.

By demonstrating resilience, leaders inspire their teams to persevere and remain committed to their shared mission.

Strategic Thinking and Foresight

Strategic thinking is the ability to anticipate future challenges and opportunities, making it a critical quality for leaders who wish to drive innovation.

Leaders with strategic foresight can evaluate the potential impact of new technologies, market trends, and industry shifts, enabling them to make informed decisions that align with the organization's long-term goals.

Strategic leaders are proactive rather than reactive, guiding their teams to take calculated steps toward innovation and growth.

By balancing short-term objectives with long-term vision, leaders create a sustainable path for innovation that can withstand the challenges of an evolving business landscape.

Empowerment and Delegation

Empowering team members is essential for fostering innovation.

Leaders who delegate effectively and trust their teams to take ownership of tasks create a sense of autonomy and accountability.

Empowered team members are more likely to take initiative, explore creative solutions, and contribute to the organization's innovation efforts.

Delegation also allows leaders to focus on high-level strategic decisions, knowing that their teams are equipped to handle the operational aspects.

By empowering their teams, leaders foster a culture of collaboration, innovation, and shared responsibility.

These leadership qualities form the foundation for driving innovation and resilience in any organization.

By embodying these traits, leaders not only inspire their teams but also create an environment where creativity, adaptability, and growth thrive.

In the Age of Innovation, effective leadership goes beyond directing tasks — it involves guiding teams toward a shared vision, fostering a culture of continuous improvement, and navigating change with confidence and empathy.

Strategies for Cultivating a Team Culture That Embraces Change and Creativity

Creating a team culture that embraces change and encourages creativity is essential for fostering innovation within an organization.

In a world where adaptability is crucial, leaders play a key role in shaping an environment where teams feel empowered to explore new ideas and tackle challenges.

Here are strategies for cultivating a team culture that is open to change and fueled by creativity.

Promote Psychological Safety

Psychological safety is the foundation of a creative, adaptable team culture.

When team members feel safe to express ideas, ask questions, and take risks without fear of judgment or retribution, they are more likely to contribute openly.

Leaders can promote psychological safety by encouraging open communication, celebrating diverse viewpoints, and handling mistakes as learning opportunities.

In an environment where people feel valued and respected, creativity flourishes, and team members are more willing to embrace change.

Encourage Collaborative Problem-Solving

Collaboration is a powerful driver of creativity and innovation.

By encouraging team members to work together on projects and brainstorm ideas, leaders create a culture of shared ownership and mutual support.

Collaborative problem-solving allows individuals to learn from each other's experiences and insights, leading to more robust and innovative solutions.

Techniques such as *design thinking workshops*, *cross-functional teams*, and *brainstorming sessions* help foster a collaborative culture where team members are motivated to work toward common goals.

Provide Opportunities for Continuous Learning

A culture that embraces change requires a commitment to continuous learning.

Leaders can support this by offering opportunities for professional development, such as workshops, online courses, and mentorship programs.

When team members have access to resources that help them build new skills and stay up-to-date with industry trends, they are more adaptable and open to change.

Continuous learning encourages curiosity, reduces resistance to new ideas, and empowers individuals to contribute innovative solutions.

Reward Innovation and Celebrate Successes

Recognizing and rewarding innovative efforts reinforces a culture that values creativity. Leaders can establish reward systems, such as bonuses, promotions, or public recognition, to celebrate team members who contribute new ideas or go above and beyond in their roles.

Celebrating both small and large successes shows the team that innovation is appreciated, building morale and motivating individuals to continue pushing boundaries.

By rewarding innovation, leaders create a positive feedback loop that encourages ongoing creativity and adaptability.

Embrace Flexible Work Structures

Flexibility is a valuable asset in a culture that embraces change.

Allowing team members to work in ways that suit their strengths and preferences, whether through flexible hours, remote work, or project-based assignments, enables them to think creatively and adapt to evolving tasks.

Flexible work structures empower team members to approach challenges in their own way, leading to fresh perspectives and innovative solutions.

By providing autonomy, leaders help foster a culture of trust, adaptability, and empowerment.

Set Clear Goals and Provide a Vision for Change

A clear vision provides a sense of purpose and direction, aligning team efforts with the organization's long-term goals.

When teams understand the reasons behind changes and the role of innovation in achieving those goals, they are more likely to embrace new ideas.

Leaders can set specific, achievable goals that highlight the importance of adaptability and creativity, showing the team how their contributions fit into the broader mission.

Clear communication of goals and vision creates a unified, purpose-driven approach to change.

Foster a Growth Mindset

A growth mindset is the belief that abilities and intelligence can be developed through effort and learning.

Leaders can cultivate a growth mindset by encouraging team members to view challenges as opportunities for growth rather than obstacles.

By promoting the idea that skills can be improved, leaders help teams become more resilient, open to feedback, and willing to take risks.

A growth mindset fosters an environment where creativity is valued, and team members feel empowered to pursue new ideas.

Involve Team Members in Decision-Making

Including team members in the decision-making process gives them a sense of ownership and commitment to the organization's goals.

When team members are involved in decisions related to projects, policies, or changes, they feel more invested in the outcome and more motivated to contribute creative ideas.

Leaders can hold regular meetings or brainstorming sessions where team members are encouraged to share their perspectives and collaborate on solutions.

Involving the team in decision-making fosters a sense of community and shared purpose.

Provide the Tools and Resources Needed for Innovation

Creativity and adaptability require the right tools and resources.

Leaders can support their teams by providing access to innovative technology, software, and research materials that enhance productivity and spark new ideas.

For example, project management tools, collaborative platforms, and brainstorming software can streamline workflows and improve communication.

By investing in tools that facilitate creativity, leaders enable their teams to explore new possibilities and approach challenges with a fresh perspective.

Lead by Example

Leaders set the tone for team culture, and their actions speak louder than words.

By demonstrating a willingness to embrace change, take risks, and approach challenges with creativity, leaders inspire their teams to do the same.

Leading by example shows the team that adaptability and innovation are valued, creating an environment where everyone feels empowered to contribute to the organization's growth.

When leaders model the behaviors they wish to see, they cultivate a team culture that is resilient, forward-thinking, and open to new ideas.

These strategies provide a roadmap for building a team culture that not only embraces change but also actively pursues creativity and innovation.

By fostering an environment where adaptability, collaboration, and continuous learning are encouraged, leaders can cultivate a resilient, high-performing team ready to meet the demands of an ever-evolving business landscape.

Chapter 5: Sustainability as a Growth Strategy

Sustainability has moved from a "nice-to-have" initiative to a core driver of business growth.

Today, integrating sustainable practices into business strategy isn't just about complying with regulations or enhancing public image — it's about building resilience, meeting consumer demands, and creating long-term value.

As global challenges like climate change, resource scarcity, and social inequity become more pressing, businesses that prioritize sustainability are better positioned to thrive in an evolving landscape.

In this chapter, we explore how sustainability can be leveraged as a growth strategy, driving innovation and strengthening a company's foundation for the future.

We'll discuss actionable insights on embedding sustainability into core business practices, from supply chain management to product development and beyond.

Additionally, we'll examine the profound benefits of sustainability, such as enhanced brand reputation, increased customer loyalty, and improved profitability over the long term.

Whether you're looking to refine your existing sustainability initiatives or build a sustainable strategy from the ground up, this chapter provides a roadmap for turning sustainability into a key component of your business's success.

Embedding Sustainability into Business Strategy

Embedding sustainability into business strategy involves a shift in how an organization approaches its operations, values, and goals.

It's more than reducing waste or using eco-friendly materials; it requires a comprehensive and integrated approach that considers the environmental, social, and economic impacts of every decision.

Here are key insights into how organizations can embed sustainability into their business strategies to foster growth and resilience.

Define a Clear Sustainability Vision and Goals

The first step in embedding sustainability into business strategy is defining a clear vision.

This vision should articulate the organization's commitment to sustainability and reflect its values. It's crucial to involve leadership and stakeholders in crafting this vision, ensuring alignment with the company's overall mission and long-term goals.

Once the vision is established, specific, measurable goals should be set.

These goals could include reducing carbon emissions, sourcing sustainable materials, or achieving zero waste in production.

By establishing a vision and goals, organizations create a roadmap for integrating sustainability into their strategy.

Incorporate Sustainability into Core Values and Culture

To truly embed sustainability, it must become part of the company's DNA. This means incorporating sustainability into core values and fostering a culture where sustainable practices are encouraged and rewarded.

Leaders play a critical role here; by modeling sustainable behaviors, they set an example for employees.

Regular training and open discussions on sustainability help to reinforce its importance within the company culture.

When sustainability becomes a shared value, employees at all levels are more likely to consider the environmental and social impacts of their actions, making sustainable practices more ingrained in daily operations.

Assess the Entire Supply Chain

Sustainability goes beyond a company's immediate operations; it extends to its entire supply chain.

A sustainable business strategy should include a thorough assessment of suppliers, manufacturers, and distribution partners to ensure alignment with the company's sustainability goals.

This can involve choosing suppliers who prioritize eco-friendly practices, reducing the environmental footprint of transportation, and using recycled or renewable materials in production.

A transparent supply chain is essential, as it allows companies to identify areas for improvement and communicate their sustainability efforts to customers.

Businesses that adopt a sustainable supply chain create a positive impact that extends beyond their own organization.

Invest in Sustainable Product Design

Products are often the most visible representation of a company's commitment to sustainability.

Designing products with sustainability in mind — such as using recyclable materials, reducing packaging waste, or extending product lifecycles — demonstrates a commitment to environmental responsibility.

Sustainable product design also involves considering the end-of-life stage, ensuring that products can be easily recycled, reused, or composted.

By investing in sustainable design, companies can appeal to environmentally conscious consumers while reducing waste and conserving resources.

Sustainable product design not only supports the company's growth goals but also enhances its reputation and competitiveness in the market.

Use Data to Drive Sustainable Decision-Making

Data is a powerful tool for measuring the impact of sustainability efforts and guiding future decisions.

Companies should track metrics related to energy consumption, waste generation, water usage, and greenhouse gas emissions to understand the effectiveness of their initiatives.

Data analytics can reveal trends and identify areas where improvements are needed, enabling companies to make informed adjustments to their sustainability strategy.

Additionally, data provides transparency, allowing organizations to communicate their progress to stakeholders and customers with credibility.

When sustainability efforts are data-driven, businesses are better equipped to achieve their goals and demonstrate accountability.

Engage with Stakeholders

Effective sustainability strategies involve collaboration with stakeholders, including employees, customers, investors, and communities.

Engaging stakeholders ensures that the company's sustainability goals reflect the values and expectations of those it serves.

Regular communication with stakeholders allows companies to receive feedback, build trust, and foster a sense of shared responsibility for sustainability.

For instance, customers may be willing to pay a premium for sustainable products, while investors may seek transparency in environmental, social, and governance (ESG) practices.

By engaging stakeholders, companies build a loyal network of supporters who are invested in the company's sustainability journey.

Align Sustainability with Innovation and Growth

Sustainability and innovation are closely connected. Companies that prioritize sustainable practices often find new opportunities for innovation, such as developing eco-friendly products, improving efficiency, and reducing costs.

Embedding sustainability into business strategy encourages creative problem-solving and can lead to breakthroughs that set a company apart from competitors.

For example, adopting circular economy principles—where products are designed for reuse, remanufacturing, or recycling—can drive sustainable growth by reducing reliance on finite resources.

Companies that align sustainability with innovation can differentiate themselves in the market and build resilience against resource scarcity.

Set Long-Term Goals and Short-Term Milestones

A sustainable business strategy requires both long-term vision and short-term milestones.

While long-term goals provide a clear direction, short-term milestones help maintain momentum and track progress.

By breaking down sustainability goals into actionable steps, companies can celebrate incremental successes, making the journey toward sustainability more tangible and achievable.

For example, a company might set a long-term goal of achieving net-zero emissions by 2030, with annual targets to reduce emissions by a certain percentage.

This approach allows for continuous improvement and keeps sustainability at the forefront of the organization's growth strategy.

Educate and Empower Employees

Employees are instrumental in driving sustainability initiatives, and they need the knowledge and resources to contribute effectively.

Providing training on sustainability practices, encouraging participation in green initiatives, and recognizing employees' efforts in promoting sustainability fosters a culture of responsibility.

Empowered employees can become advocates for sustainability within and beyond the organization, helping to build momentum for sustainable growth.

Education also equips employees to make sustainable choices in their roles, whether by reducing waste, conserving energy, or supporting sustainable suppliers.

Measure, Report, and Communicate Sustainability Efforts

Transparency is essential for a credible sustainability strategy.

Companies should regularly measure and report their sustainability efforts, providing updates on progress toward goals.

Public sustainability reports, environmental impact statements, or regular updates on the company's website build trust with stakeholders.

Clear, honest communication about both achievements and challenges helps stakeholders understand the company's commitment to sustainability.

By sharing progress and being transparent, organizations can strengthen their brand reputation and inspire loyalty among customers, investors, and the public.

By embedding sustainability into every facet of the business, companies can achieve meaningful, long-term growth.

These insights provide a roadmap for creating a sustainability strategy that not only drives profitability but also supports environmental stewardship and social responsibility.

Benefits of Sustainable Practices for Brand Reputation, Customer Loyalty, and Long-Term Profitability

The benefits of sustainable practices extend beyond environmental impact; they enhance brand reputation, foster customer loyalty, and support long-term profitability.

In today's conscious consumer market, businesses that prioritize sustainability can achieve a competitive edge and secure a lasting place in the industry.

Here's a closer look at how sustainable practices contribute to these key areas.

Enhanced Brand Reputation

In an age where consumers are increasingly aware of environmental and social issues, a commitment to sustainability is a powerful differentiator.

Companies that integrate sustainable practices into their brand strategy are seen as responsible, forward-thinking, and trustworthy.

This positive perception strengthens brand reputation, helping companies stand out in a competitive market.

When customers view a brand as environmentally and socially responsible, they are more likely to engage, advocate, and become loyal patrons.

A strong reputation for sustainability also attracts partnerships, as businesses and investors increasingly seek to collaborate with organizations that align with their values.

Building Customer Loyalty

Sustainable practices are particularly valued by today's consumers, who often make purchasing decisions based on a company's environmental and ethical commitments.

Brands that demonstrate sustainability efforts, such as reducing plastic use or supporting fair labor practices, appeal to consumers who prioritize responsible shopping.

When customers feel that their purchases contribute to positive environmental and social outcomes, they are more likely to remain loyal to the brand.

Sustainable practices thus become a cornerstone of customer loyalty, providing consumers with an added layer of trust and satisfaction in their brand choices.

Long-Term Profitability Through Cost Savings

While sustainability efforts may require an initial investment, they can lead to substantial cost savings over time.

For instance, energy-efficient processes reduce utility bills, while waste reduction initiatives decrease disposal costs.

By minimizing resource usage and streamlining operations, sustainable practices enhance profitability.

Additionally, companies that invest in sustainable practices are better prepared for potential regulatory changes related to environmental standards, avoiding costly compliance penalties.

Sustainable business practices thus offer a pathway to long-term profitability, enabling companies to save on operational costs while contributing positively to the environment.

Increased Market Share and Consumer Trust

A commitment to sustainability can expand a company's market share by appealing to a growing demographic of eco-conscious consumers.

As awareness of environmental issues rises, more consumers are willing to pay a premium for sustainable products and services.

Companies that prioritize sustainability tap into this market demand, attracting new customers and expanding their reach.

Consumer trust is also strengthened, as sustainability fosters transparency and accountability.

By providing clear information about sustainable practices, companies build relationships based on trust and shared values, increasing customer retention and expanding their market presence.

Resilience Against Market Fluctuations

Sustainable practices contribute to organizational resilience by mitigating risks associated with resource scarcity and market volatility.

For example, companies that rely on renewable energy sources are less vulnerable to fluctuations in fossil fuel prices, while those that adopt water conservation measures are better prepared for periods of drought.

Sustainable sourcing practices reduce dependency on non-renewable resources, shielding the company from supply chain disruptions.

By investing in sustainability, companies build resilience that enables them to weather external shocks, ensuring steady growth even in unpredictable market conditions.

Attracting and Retaining Talent

In addition to customers, sustainability is a major draw for employees, especially millennials and Gen Z professionals who value purpose-driven work.

Companies with strong sustainability practices are seen as desirable workplaces, attracting individuals who want to make a positive impact through their careers.

Employees are more likely to stay with organizations that align with their values, reducing turnover and fostering a committed workforce.

Sustainable practices thus become a factor in talent acquisition and retention, helping companies attract motivated, values-aligned employees who are committed to the company's mission.

Access to Capital and Investment Opportunities

Investors increasingly prioritize Environmental, Social, and Governance (ESG) criteria when evaluating companies.

Businesses that demonstrate a commitment to sustainability are more likely to attract investment from funds and institutions focused on ESG principles.

Sustainable practices signal to investors that the company is managing risks responsibly and has a long-term growth strategy.

Access to capital for sustainability-driven initiatives provides companies with resources to expand, innovate, and further enhance their operations, supporting long-term growth and profitability.

Regulatory Compliance and Risk Mitigation

Adopting sustainable practices prepares companies for compliance with evolving environmental regulations.

Governments around the world are introducing stricter standards related to carbon emissions, waste disposal, and resource conservation.

Companies that proactively implement sustainable practices are better positioned to meet these standards, avoiding the financial risks associated with non-compliance.

In addition, sustainability efforts reduce exposure to legal liabilities related to environmental or social issues, further mitigating operational risks and safeguarding the company's reputation.

Strengthening Community and Social Impact

Sustainability goes beyond environmental initiatives; it encompasses social responsibility, such as supporting local communities, fair labor practices, and ethical sourcing.

Companies that engage in meaningful social initiatives build strong relationships with their communities, enhancing brand reputation and customer loyalty.

that adopt water conservation measures are better prepared for periods of drought.

Sustainable sourcing practices reduce dependency on non-renewable resources, shielding the company from supply chain disruptions.

By investing in sustainability, companies build resilience that enables them to weather external shocks, ensuring steady growth even in unpredictable market conditions.

Attracting and Retaining Talent

In addition to customers, sustainability is a major draw for employees, especially millennials and Gen Z professionals who value purpose-driven work.

Companies with strong sustainability practices are seen as desirable workplaces, attracting individuals who want to make a positive impact through their careers.

Employees are more likely to stay with organizations that align with their values, reducing turnover and fostering a committed workforce.

Sustainable practices thus become a factor in talent acquisition and retention, helping companies attract motivated, values-aligned employees who are committed to the company's mission.

Access to Capital and Investment Opportunities

Investors increasingly prioritize Environmental, Social, and Governance (ESG) criteria when evaluating companies.

Businesses that demonstrate a commitment to sustainability are more likely to attract investment from funds and institutions focused on ESG principles.

Sustainable practices signal to investors that the company is managing risks responsibly and has a long-term growth strategy.

Access to capital for sustainability-driven initiatives provides companies with resources to expand, innovate, and further enhance their operations, supporting long-term growth and profitability.

Regulatory Compliance and Risk Mitigation

Adopting sustainable practices prepares companies for compliance with evolving environmental regulations.

Governments around the world are introducing stricter standards related to carbon emissions, waste disposal, and resource conservation.

Companies that proactively implement sustainable practices are better positioned to meet these standards, avoiding the financial risks associated with non-compliance.

In addition, sustainability efforts reduce exposure to legal liabilities related to environmental or social issues, further mitigating operational risks and safeguarding the company's reputation.

Strengthening Community and Social Impact

Sustainability goes beyond environmental initiatives; it encompasses social responsibility, such as supporting local communities, fair labor practices, and ethical sourcing.

Companies that engage in meaningful social initiatives build strong relationships with their communities, enhancing brand reputation and customer loyalty.

Socially responsible practices demonstrate a company's commitment to making a positive impact, fostering goodwill and strengthening community ties.

This commitment contributes to a holistic brand image, attracting consumers and partners who value ethical, community-oriented businesses.

Innovation and Competitive Advantage

Sustainability encourages innovation as companies seek new ways to reduce environmental impact and enhance efficiency.

By investing in research and development for eco-friendly products, sustainable packaging, and resource-efficient processes, companies can create unique offerings that differentiate them in the marketplace.

Innovation driven by sustainability not only improves operational efficiency but also positions companies as leaders in their industry.

Sustainable innovation provides a competitive advantage, attracting customers, investors, and partners who value progressive, forward-thinking brands.

These benefits illustrate how sustainable practices contribute to a company's success, building a brand that is trusted, admired, and resilient.

By embracing sustainability as a growth strategy, businesses can achieve long-term profitability while making a positive impact on the world.

Chapter 6: Preparing your Organization for Innovation Readiness

In a rapidly evolving marketplace, the ability to innovate is no longer just an advantage — it's a necessity for survival and growth.

However, true innovation readiness goes beyond brainstorming new ideas; it involves establishing the right structures, processes, and culture that allow an organization to adapt, experiment, and transform continuously.

Preparing for innovation means assessing an organization's current state, identifying strengths and areas for improvement, and developing a solid foundation that supports creative thinking and agile responses to change.

This chapter explores the essential steps for assessing and enhancing your organization's readiness for innovation. We'll examine how to evaluate existing capabilities, align resources, and foster a culture that encourages curiosity and resilience.

Additionally, we'll offer practical tips for building organizational structures and processes that support sustainable growth, ensuring that your teams are equipped not only to generate innovative ideas but also to bring them to life effectively.

By embedding innovation readiness into the core of your organization, you can create a dynamic environment that's prepared to seize opportunities, tackle challenges, and adapt to an ever-changing world.

Steps to Assess and Enhance Organizational Readiness for Innovation

Organizational readiness for innovation is the foundation upon which successful, sustainable growth is built.

It involves evaluating the current state of the organization's capabilities, processes, culture, and resources to determine its ability to support and sustain innovation.

By identifying strengths and addressing gaps, leaders can build an environment that nurtures creativity, agility, and resilience.

Here's a step-by-step approach to assessing and enhancing your organization's innovation readiness.

Conduct an Innovation Readiness Assessment

The first step in preparing your organization for innovation is conducting a comprehensive readiness assessment.

This involves evaluating key areas such as leadership support, resource allocation, employee skills, and cultural alignment with innovation goals.

A readiness assessment can be done through surveys, interviews, or workshops with employees and stakeholders to gain insights into the current state of innovation.

The results of this assessment provide a baseline understanding of the organization's strengths and areas for improvement, helping leaders identify where to focus their efforts in building innovation capacity.

Evaluate Leadership Commitment to Innovation

Leadership commitment is crucial to fostering an innovation-ready organization. Leaders must not only support innovation verbally but also demonstrate commitment through their actions.

Assess the degree to which leadership actively promotes and participates in innovation initiatives.

This includes evaluating leaders' openness to new ideas, willingness to allocate resources, and readiness to support calculated risk-taking.

Leaders who are visible champions of innovation inspire confidence and motivation among employees, creating a top-down culture that values experimentation and continuous improvement.

Assess Resource Availability and Allocation

Innovation requires dedicated resources — both financial and human. Assess whether the organization has allocated sufficient resources to support innovation efforts.

This includes budget for research and development, access to necessary tools and technology, and time for employees to work on creative projects.

Resource constraints can hinder innovation, so it's essential to evaluate and, if needed, reallocate resources to ensure that teams have what they need to experiment and explore new ideas.

An organization that prioritizes resource allocation for innovation demonstrates its commitment to fostering a culture of creativity.

Identify and Develop Skills for Innovation

Innovation requires specific skills, such as creative problem-solving, critical thinking, and adaptability. Assess the skill levels of employees across departments to identify any gaps that may limit the organization's ability to innovate effectively.

Skills assessments, training programs, and development workshops can be valuable tools in building innovation capabilities.

By investing in upskilling and reskilling, organizations equip their teams with the competencies needed to generate and implement new ideas.

Encouraging continuous learning also creates a culture that embraces change, preparing employees to take on the challenges of a dynamic market.

Evaluate Organizational Structure and Decision-Making Processes

An organization's structure can either facilitate or hinder innovation.

Hierarchical structures with rigid decision-making processes can slow down innovation, while more agile, flexible structures enable faster responses to change.

Assess the current organizational structure and decision-making pathways to determine whether they support or restrict innovation.

Consider implementing flatter structures, cross-functional teams, and decentralized decision-making to promote collaboration and speed up the innovation process.

When employees feel empowered to make decisions and experiment within their roles, they are more likely to contribute to innovative efforts.

Examine the Culture of Risk-Taking and Experimentation

Innovation thrives in a culture that values risk-taking and sees failure as a learning opportunity.

Evaluate the organization's attitude toward risk and failure by examining whether employees feel safe to share ideas, experiment, and make mistakes without fear of negative repercussions.

To cultivate a culture of innovation, leaders must encourage a growth mindset, where setbacks are viewed as opportunities for improvement.

Recognize and reward employees who take thoughtful risks, reinforcing the idea that experimentation is a valuable part of the innovation journey.

Align Innovation Goals with Business Strategy

Innovation readiness is most effective when it aligns with the organization's broader business strategy.

Review the organization's strategic goals and ensure that innovation initiatives support these objectives.

By aligning innovation with core business goals, leaders create a clear purpose for innovation efforts, making it easier to prioritize projects, allocate resources, and gain stakeholder buy-in.

An organization that integrates innovation into its strategic plan sends a message that creativity and adaptability are essential to its future success.

Foster a Collaborative Environment

Innovation often occurs at the intersection of different perspectives and expertise.

Assess the organization's level of cross-functional collaboration and communication to determine whether it encourages idea sharing across teams.

Creating opportunities for collaboration, such as cross-departmental projects, idea-sharing sessions, and collaborative problem-solving, helps break down silos and generates fresh ideas.

A collaborative environment promotes knowledge exchange, fosters diverse viewpoints, and enhances the overall capacity for innovation.

Establish Metrics to Measure Innovation Readiness and Success

To ensure that innovation efforts are effective, organizations need measurable metrics that track progress and outcomes.

Establishing Key Performance Indicators (KPIs) for innovation readiness allows leaders to monitor improvements over time.

Metrics may include the number of new ideas generated, time to market for new products, and employee engagement in innovation initiatives.

Regularly reviewing these metrics helps leaders identify areas where the organization excels and areas that may require additional focus, ensuring continuous growth in innovation readiness.

Communicate and Reinforce the Innovation Vision

Communication is essential to building a culture that values innovation.

Clearly articulate the organization's innovation vision, goals, and progress to employees at all levels.

This includes sharing success stories, recognizing contributions, and providing updates on ongoing initiatives.

Regular communication reinforces the importance of innovation, keeps employees informed, and fosters a sense of shared purpose.

By consistently highlighting the value of innovation, leaders create a culture that encourages employees to contribute ideas, collaborate, and work toward a common goal.

Tips for Ensuring that Structures, Processes, and Culture Support Growth and Adaptability

Creating a robust foundation for innovation requires aligning organizational structures, processes, and culture to support growth and adaptability.

When these elements are designed to foster creativity and agility, they empower teams to respond to change and drive sustainable success.

Here are essential tips for building structures, processes, and a culture that supports innovation readiness.

Adopt an Agile Organizational Structure

Traditional hierarchical structures can stifle innovation, as they often involve rigid chains of command and slow decision-making.

Consider adopting an agile structure that emphasizes flexibility, collaboration, and empowerment at every level.

Agile organizations often use cross-functional teams that work autonomously, enabling faster responses to challenges and opportunities.

By promoting a flatter structure, leaders can create an environment where information flows freely, ideas are shared openly, and teams can adapt quickly to changes in the market.

Implement Flexible, Adaptive Processes

Standardized processes are essential for consistency, but overly rigid procedures can hinder innovation.

Create processes that are flexible and adaptable, allowing teams to modify workflows when needed.

For example, iterative project management methodologies such as Agile or Lean provide a framework for continuous improvement, enabling teams to test, learn, and refine ideas rapidly.

Adaptive processes create room for experimentation, helping teams learn from each iteration and make data-driven adjustments.

Encourage Open Communication and Knowledge Sharing

Open communication is vital for creating an innovation-ready culture. Establish channels where team members can share insights, ask questions, and offer feedback without barriers.

Collaborative tools, such as shared digital platforms, encourage knowledge sharing and foster a sense of community.

By promoting transparent communication, leaders enable employees to stay informed, gain diverse perspectives, and feel more engaged in the innovation process.

Provide Access to Necessary Resources and Tools

Innovation requires resources, from access to cutting-edge technology to time allocated for creative exploration.

Ensure that employees have the tools they need to develop and test new ideas. Invest in technology platforms that facilitate collaboration, project management, and data analysis.

Offering dedicated innovation resources, such as budget for prototyping or time for brainstorming sessions, empowers teams to pursue creative solutions and explore new possibilities.

Incentivize and Reward Innovation Efforts

Recognizing and rewarding innovation is essential for building a culture that values creativity and adaptability. Establish incentives that encourage employees to share ideas, experiment, and contribute to innovation initiatives.

This could involve recognition programs, monetary rewards, or opportunities for career advancement.

By acknowledging innovative efforts, leaders reinforce the importance of creativity and motivate employees to continuously seek ways to improve.

Empower Teams to Make Decisions

Decision-making autonomy is a key factor in fostering innovation. Empower teams to make decisions within their areas of responsibility, reducing reliance on top-down directives.

When employees feel trusted to make choices and take ownership of their projects, they are more likely to take risks and pursue new ideas.

Decision-making autonomy enables teams to act swiftly, experiment, and learn from their experiences, building confidence in their ability to drive innovation.

Establish Clear Innovation Goals and Objectives

Setting clear innovation goals provides direction and aligns teams with the organization's broader strategy.

Define specific objectives for innovation, such as launching a certain number of new products annually or reducing production costs through process improvements.

Clear goals give employees a target to strive for and help prioritize innovation initiatives. Regularly reviewing progress toward these goals allows leaders to celebrate successes and make necessary adjustments.

Foster a Culture of Continuous Learning

A growth-oriented culture embraces continuous learning and encourages employees to expand their skills.

Provide opportunities for professional development, such as workshops, online courses, or mentorship programs.

When teams are equipped with new skills and knowledge, they are more adaptable and open to change.

Leaders can model continuous learning by sharing their own development experiences, creating an environment where learning is valued and celebrated.

Encourage Experimentation and Accept Failure as Learning

Innovation involves risk, and not every idea will succeed. Encourage teams to experiment and view failure as a learning opportunity.

By normalizing failure, leaders create a safe space where employees feel comfortable exploring new ideas without fear of repercussions.

Establishing a framework for evaluating failures, identifying lessons learned, and applying these insights to future projects enables teams to innovate more effectively and sustainably.

Integrate Sustainability and Social Responsibility

Today's employees and customers value organizations that prioritize sustainability and social impact.

Integrating these values into innovation initiatives can enhance employee engagement and strengthen the organization's commitment to ethical practices.

Leaders can encourage teams to consider environmental impact, resource efficiency, and social responsibility when developing new ideas. Sustainability not only supports the organization's growth objectives but also fosters a sense of purpose and responsibility within the team.

By aligning structures, processes, and culture to support innovation readiness, leaders create an organization that is agile, adaptable, and capable of thriving in a dynamic market.

These tips provide a roadmap for fostering a work environment where creativity and resilience flourish, enabling teams to tackle challenges and seize opportunities with confidence and purpose.

Chapter 7: Purpose-Driven Innovation Aligning Growth with Core Values

In an increasingly conscious marketplace, purpose-driven innovation has emerged as a powerful strategy for aligning growth with core values.

This approach goes beyond profits, focusing on creating solutions that benefit society, respect the environment, and resonate deeply with customers and stakeholders.

Purpose-driven innovation enables companies to address complex challenges while remaining true to their mission, setting them apart in an environment where consumers and investors alike seek brands that stand for something meaningful.

In this chapter, we'll explore the principles of purpose-driven innovation and examine how aligning growth initiatives with core values can positively shape brand identity.

From enhancing customer loyalty to attracting top talent, a purpose-oriented approach to innovation strengthens the organization's foundation and long-term resilience.

Through real-world case studies, we'll look at how leading companies are successfully integrating purpose with innovation to make a measurable difference in their industries and communities.

Whether you're refining an existing strategy or building one from scratch, this chapter provides a roadmap for embedding purpose at the heart of innovation, ensuring that each step forward reflects a commitment to values and meaningful impact.

Purpose-Driven Innovation and Its Impact on Brand Identity

Purpose-driven innovation is a strategic approach that combines the drive for growth with a commitment to creating positive, meaningful impact on society and the environment.

It's a philosophy that emphasizes that innovation should do more than just meet market demands — it should align with the organization's core values and contribute to a greater good.

This type of innovation has gained traction in recent years, as consumers, employees, and investors increasingly expect companies to stand for more than just profits.

By aligning innovation with purpose, organizations can differentiate themselves, foster loyalty, and build a strong, authentic brand identity.

Understanding Purpose-Driven Innovation

Purpose-driven innovation is built on the principle that businesses have a responsibility to consider the broader impact of their actions.

Rather than focusing solely on financial performance, purpose-driven companies prioritize initiatives that create social and environmental value.

This approach often involves addressing issues such as sustainability, community welfare, and ethical practices, while simultaneously pursuing innovation that supports business growth.

Purpose-driven innovation can manifest in various forms, from developing eco-friendly products to supporting fair trade practices and reducing carbon footprints.

The ultimate goal is to create solutions that benefit both the business and the wider world.

One of the key aspects of purpose-driven innovation is that it requires alignment between an organization's values and its growth objectives.

For this to happen, purpose must be ingrained in the company's mission, culture, and decision-making processes.

Leaders and employees alike should be clear on what the company stands for and how it aims to make a positive impact.

This clarity helps guide innovation efforts in a way that reinforces the company's purpose, making each project, product, or initiative an opportunity to demonstrate the brand's commitment to its core values.

The Impact of Purpose on Brand Identity

A brand's identity is defined by more than its logo or tagline — it's shaped by the values, beliefs, and principles that underpin every action.

Purpose-driven innovation plays a significant role in shaping brand identity because it conveys authenticity and integrity.

One Step at a Time

When a company innovates with purpose, it sends a clear message to customers, employees, and stakeholders that it is committed to making a difference.

This message builds trust and credibility, as consumers are more likely to support brands that reflect their own values and contribute to the betterment of society.

Purpose-driven innovation can significantly enhance brand reputation, as it demonstrates a company's commitment to issues that matter to its customers.

In an age where consumers are increasingly conscious of social and environmental issues, brands that take a stand on these matters are seen as forward-thinking and trustworthy.

This positive perception extends beyond customers to employees, who are often more engaged and motivated to work for a company that shares their values.

A strong brand identity rooted in purpose can thus drive loyalty, attract talent, and create a sense of community around the brand.

Building Customer Loyalty Through Purpose

Purpose-driven innovation appeals to consumers on a personal level, creating emotional connections that go beyond the product or service itself.

Customers today want to feel that their purchases contribute to positive change, whether that's reducing environmental impact, supporting fair labor, or promoting social justice.

Brands that align with these values resonate deeply with consumers, building loyalty and advocacy. Purpose-driven innovation offers a way to meet these expectations, turning customers into brand ambassadors who support and advocate for the brand's mission.

For example, a company that develops sustainable packaging not only reduces its environmental footprint but also appeals to eco-conscious consumers.

Customers who align with the brand's values are more likely to remain loyal, even in the face of competition.

By building a strong connection based on shared values, companies can foster long-term relationships with customers who see their purchase decisions as a reflection of their personal beliefs.

Differentiating in a Competitive Market

In crowded markets, differentiation is key to standing out. Purpose-driven innovation provides a unique way for brands to distinguish themselves by showcasing their commitment to social and environmental causes.

While product features and pricing are important, purpose-driven companies differentiate themselves through their values and ethical stance.

This approach can be especially effective in industries where consumer choices are influenced by values, such as food and beverage, fashion, and beauty.

By incorporating purpose into innovation, companies position themselves as leaders who are not only innovative but also principled, setting themselves apart from competitors.

Attracting and Retaining Top Talent

Purpose-driven innovation doesn't just resonate with customers; it's also a powerful tool for attracting and retaining talent.

Today's workforce, particularly millennials and Gen Z, is drawn to companies that are committed to making a positive impact.

Employees want to work for organizations that align with their own values and provide meaningful, purpose-driven work.

By incorporating purpose into innovation, companies create an environment where employees feel motivated to contribute to projects that have a real impact on the world.

This sense of purpose enhances job satisfaction, reduces turnover, and attracts talented individuals who are passionate about making a difference.

Creating a Lasting Legacy

Purpose-driven innovation allows companies to build a legacy that goes beyond profits.

By aligning growth initiatives with core values, organizations can create long-term impact that resonates with customers, employees, and communities.

A brand that is known for its commitment to purpose leaves a lasting impression on the industry and society.

This legacy is a powerful form of brand equity, as it builds goodwill and strengthens the brand's reputation over time.

When purpose is embedded in innovation, companies not only achieve sustainable growth but also contribute to a future that reflects their ideals and values.

Challenges and Considerations

While purpose-driven innovation offers significant benefits, it also requires commitment, transparency, and consistency.

Organizations must be prepared to back their values with action, as consumers and stakeholders expect authenticity.

This means that purpose-driven innovation cannot be a one-time initiative; it must be part of the company's ongoing strategy.

Additionally, purpose-driven innovation requires regular communication with stakeholders to ensure that the brand's efforts are understood and appreciated. Transparency is key, as consumers expect brands to be open about their initiatives, goals, and challenges.

In summary, purpose-driven innovation strengthens brand identity by aligning growth with core values. It transforms a brand into a symbol of integrity, trust, and responsibility, fostering loyalty and building a community of like-minded customers, employees, and stakeholders.

By defining a purpose that guides innovation, companies can create lasting value that goes beyond the bottom line, enhancing their reputation, building resilience, and leaving a positive impact on the world.

Case Studies and Examples of Companies Leading with Purpose

Purpose-driven innovation has been successfully adopted by companies across various industries, demonstrating how aligning growth with core values can lead to meaningful impact and brand success.

Here are some inspiring examples of companies that have embedded purpose into their innovation strategies, creating value for both their business and society.

Patagonia: Environmental Stewardship and Ethical Business Practices

Patagonia, the outdoor apparel company, is a prime example of purpose-driven innovation.

The company has built its brand around environmental stewardship, with a commitment to sustainability that goes beyond simply selling products.

Patagonia encourages customers to repair and reuse their gear, even offering repair services and promoting secondhand sales through its "Worn Wear" initiative.

This approach reduces waste and reinforces Patagonia's commitment to environmental responsibility.

In addition, Patagonia has pledged to donate a percentage of its profits to environmental causes, supporting conservation efforts and climate activism.

By aligning its growth strategy with environmental values, Patagonia has built a loyal customer base that resonates with its mission.

This commitment to purpose has not only strengthened the brand's reputation but also differentiated it in the competitive outdoor apparel market.

Unilever: Sustainable Living Plan

Unilever, a global consumer goods company, has demonstrated purpose-driven innovation through its Sustainable Living Plan, which aims to decouple business growth from environmental impact while increasing positive social impact.

Unilever's brands, such as Dove, Ben & Jerry's, and Seventh Generation, have incorporated sustainability into their core values, addressing issues like plastic waste, fair trade, and climate change.

For instance, Seventh Generation focuses on producing eco-friendly household products, while Ben & Jerry's actively campaigns for climate justice.

The Sustainable Living Plan has helped Unilever reduce its environmental footprint, enhance brand loyalty, and attract socially conscious consumers.

By embedding sustainability into its innovation strategy, Unilever has strengthened its brand identity as a company committed to responsible business practices, creating a positive impact on society while achieving long-term growth.

Tesla: Advancing Clean Energy Solutions

Tesla has positioned itself as a leader in sustainable innovation by focusing on electric vehicles, renewable energy, and reducing dependence on fossil fuels.

Tesla's mission, "to accelerate the world's transition to sustainable energy," drives its innovation strategy, resulting in products like electric vehicles, solar energy solutions, and energy storage systems.

By aligning its growth with the goal of environmental sustainability, Tesla has not only built a loyal customer base but also inspired a movement toward clean energy in the automotive and energy industries.

Tesla's purpose-driven innovation has disrupted traditional industries, setting new standards for sustainability and inspiring other companies to adopt environmentally friendly practices.

The company's success demonstrates the power of purpose-driven innovation to create a lasting impact, influence market trends, and build a brand identity associated with positive change.

The Body Shop: Ethical Sourcing and Social Responsibility

The Body Shop, a cosmetics and skincare brand, has long been recognized for its commitment to ethical sourcing, animal welfare, and social responsibility.

The company pioneered cruelty-free products, advocating against animal testing and supporting fair trade practices with its suppliers.

The Body Shop's innovation strategy emphasizes transparency, sustainability, and social impact, ensuring that its products are made with ethically sourced ingredients and environmentally friendly practices.

By prioritizing purpose-driven innovation, The Body Shop has built a brand that resonates with consumers who value ethical and sustainable products.

This commitment to purpose has fostered customer loyalty and set a standard for other brands in the beauty industry to follow, proving that purpose-driven practices can be a powerful differentiator.

Warby Parker: Social Impact Through Vision Accessibility

Warby Parker, an eyewear company, has incorporated social impact into its business model with a "buy a pair, give a pair" program.

For every pair of glasses sold, the company donates a pair to someone in need, improving access to vision care for underserved communities.

This purpose-driven initiative has become central to Warby Parker's brand identity, aligning its growth with a meaningful mission.

Warby Parker's commitment to social impact has attracted customers who appreciate its efforts to make a difference.

This purpose-driven innovation strategy has helped the company build a loyal customer base, achieve rapid growth, and create a positive reputation in the eyewear industry.

Warby Parker's success illustrates how purpose-driven innovation can drive brand loyalty while addressing social challenges.

BrewDog: Environmental sustainability and carbon reduction

BrewDog, a UK-based craft brewery, has become a leading example of purpose-driven innovation in the beverage industry, particularly with its focus on environmental sustainability and carbon reduction.

Founded in 2007, BrewDog has grown from a small craft brewery to an internationally recognized brand, known for its commitment to sustainability as much as for its innovative craft beers.

In 2020, BrewDog announced its "carbon negative" commitment, making it the first international beer brand to remove more carbon dioxide from the atmosphere than it emits.

BrewDog launched its sustainability initiative by investing in carbon reduction projects, including planting forests, conserving biodiversity, and capturing carbon emissions from its brewing processes.

The company has even purchased land in the Scottish Highlands, creating the "BrewDog Forest," a 2,050-acre forest that will remove significant amounts of CO_2 from the atmosphere over time.

BrewDog's commitment to sustainability extends to its operations and product packaging as well. The company has transitioned to using renewable energy in its breweries, dropped single-use plastic packaging, and introduced sustainable packaging alternatives.

BrewDog's bars and breweries also aim for zero-waste operations by promoting recycling and circular economy principles.

This purpose-driven innovation strategy has strengthened BrewDog's brand identity as an environmentally conscious company, appealing to eco-minded consumers who support its efforts to address climate change.

By integrating sustainability deeply into its business model, BrewDog has managed to differentiate itself in the highly competitive craft beer market, enhancing brand loyalty and attracting customers who prioritize environmental impact.

BrewDog's success demonstrates that purpose-driven innovation can foster growth and long-term resilience while contributing positively to the planet.

IKEA: Sustainability, circular economy, and social responsibility

IKEA, the globally renowned Swedish furniture retailer, has embedded purpose-driven innovation into its business strategy with a focus on sustainability and the circular economy.

IKEA's mission, "to create a better everyday life for the many people," extends beyond affordability and accessibility — it incorporates environmental and social impact, driving a range of purpose-driven initiatives.

One of IKEA's standout innovations is its commitment to the circular economy. IKEA has pledged to become fully circular by 2030, aiming to design all products using renewable or recyclable materials.

This means that products must be easy to repair, reuse, or recycle, thus reducing waste and extending product life cycles.

The company's circular model also includes buy-back and resale programs, where customers can return used furniture, which IKEA refurbishes and resells at a reduced price. This initiative supports sustainability while making furniture accessible to a wider audience.

IKEA has also invested in renewable energy sources, with most of its stores running on renewable electricity. The company has installed solar panels on many of its locations and is aiming to produce as much renewable energy as it consumes by 2025.

Furthermore, IKEA has made strides in eliminating single-use plastics and has launched several eco-friendly product lines made from sustainable materials like bamboo and recycled wood.

In addition to environmental sustainability, IKEA emphasizes social responsibility. The company's supply chain includes partnerships with artisans and cooperatives around the world, providing fair wages and supporting communities.

IKEA also works on empowering refugees through job creation and training programs as part of its commitment to positive social impact.

Through purpose-driven innovation, IKEA has enhanced its brand reputation as a leader in sustainable retailing.

By aligning growth with environmental and social goals, IKEA has attracted a loyal customer base that values the company's commitment to positive impact.

IKEA's approach exemplifies how purpose-driven innovation can contribute to sustainable growth, inspiring both customers and competitors to adopt a more sustainable way of doing business.

These case studies demonstrate how purpose-driven innovation can redefine brand identity, strengthen customer loyalty, and contribute to long-term growth.

By aligning growth initiatives with core values, these companies have created brands that resonate deeply with consumers, inspire loyalty, and set an example for others to follow.

Purpose-driven innovation offers a pathway to meaningful impact, showing that businesses can achieve success while making a positive difference in the world.

Chapter 8: Building a Roadmap for the New Year and Beyond

Creating a strategic roadmap is essential for guiding your organization's efforts and aligning teams around a common vision for growth and innovation.

As we approach the new year, businesses face an increasingly complex landscape shaped by emerging technologies, sustainability demands, and changing consumer expectations.

To navigate this environment effectively, leaders need a well-structured roadmap that not only outlines key objectives but also establishes a clear, actionable path to achieve them.

In this chapter, we'll explore the fundamentals of building a strategic roadmap that serves as a blueprint for your organization's priorities and ambitions.

From setting quarterly goals to establishing measurable milestones, we provide a step-by-step guide for developing a roadmap that reflects both your short-term objectives and long-term vision.

Additionally, we introduce practical tools, including a customizable roadmap template, quarterly goal-setting techniques, and actionable steps to keep teams focused and motivated.

Whether you're fine-tuning existing strategies or building new ones, this chapter equips you with the resources needed to navigate the new year and beyond with clarity and confidence.

Guidance on Creating a Strategic Roadmap for the New Year

Creating a strategic roadmap is a crucial step in turning an organization's vision into a series of actionable steps.

A roadmap not only helps teams stay aligned on goals but also provides a clear path to navigate the year ahead.

With the new year on the horizon, the need for a cohesive, forward-looking plan has never been greater.

Here's a guide to creating a strategic roadmap that prepares your organization to adapt, grow, and innovate in the coming year.

Define Your Vision and Objectives

The first step in building a strategic roadmap is clarifying your organization's vision and overarching objectives.

A vision provides direction and establishes the foundation for all activities within the organization.

Begin by asking critical questions: Where do you see your organization at the end of the coming year? What major goals do you want to accomplish?

Identifying these high-level objectives enables leaders to create a roadmap that aligns with the company's purpose and long-term aspirations.

Once the vision is established, break it down into specific objectives. For example, if your vision includes becoming a leader in sustainable products, your objectives could include developing eco-friendly product lines, reducing waste in production, and expanding your customer base in green markets.

Having clearly defined objectives enables you to set realistic goals and metrics for measuring progress throughout the year.

Conduct a SWOT Analysis

Before diving into goal-setting, conduct a SWOT (Strengths, Weaknesses, Opportunities, Threats) analysis to evaluate the organization's internal and external factors.

Strengths and weaknesses represent internal capabilities, such as resources, expertise, and operational efficiency, while opportunities and threats represent external factors, such as market trends, competition, and regulatory changes.

By conducting a SWOT analysis, you gain insights into potential challenges and areas of growth that may impact your roadmap.

This analysis also helps identify priorities and focus areas, ensuring that the roadmap leverages the organization's strengths and addresses potential vulnerabilities.

Establish SMART Goals

SMART goals (Specific, Measurable, Achievable, Relevant, Time-bound) provide a structured way to set actionable, realistic objectives.

Each goal in your roadmap should be specific and have measurable outcomes to track progress.

For example, instead of setting a broad goal like "improve customer satisfaction", define it as "increase customer satisfaction scores by 10% by the end of Q2 through enhanced support and feedback mechanisms".

SMART goals allow teams to understand exactly what is expected, how success will be measured, and when milestones should be achieved.

This clarity reduces ambiguity and fosters a sense of accountability within the team. Establishing SMART goals also ensures that each objective is aligned with broader strategic priorities.

Prioritize Initiatives and Milestones

Not all initiatives can be accomplished simultaneously, so prioritizing is essential for an effective roadmap.

Start by identifying key initiatives that have the highest potential for impact and align most closely with your objectives.

Break each initiative down into milestones – smaller, manageable steps that mark progress toward the larger goal.

Milestones help keep teams motivated and ensure that the organization remains on track to meet its objectives.

When prioritizing, consider the resources required for each initiative, potential obstacles, and dependencies.

This evaluation enables leaders to allocate resources efficiently, avoid bottlenecks, and make adjustments as needed.

By focusing on high-priority initiatives, the organization can achieve significant progress without spreading resources too thinly.

Allocate Resources and Set a Budget

Effective resource allocation is crucial for any strategic roadmap.

Determine the budget, personnel, technology, and other resources needed for each initiative.

Resource planning allows you to identify potential gaps, avoid resource shortages, and ensure that each project is fully supported.

Set a budget for each initiative, keeping in mind factors like projected returns, risk level, and alignment with strategic goals.

Regularly reviewing resource allocation throughout the year allows the organization to make adjustments based on project progress, unexpected challenges, or new opportunities.

Assign Responsibilities and Build Accountability

Every goal and milestone in the roadmap should have a clear owner.

Assigning responsibilities ensures that each task is managed and that accountability is maintained at every level.

When team members know their roles and understand how their work contributes to the overall roadmap, they're more likely to stay engaged and motivated.

Additionally, establish checkpoints for accountability, such as regular progress reviews and performance evaluations.

These checkpoints help teams stay on course and make adjustments as needed, creating a culture of ownership and responsibility.

Set Up Tracking and Reporting Mechanisms

To monitor progress effectively, establish tracking and reporting mechanisms that provide real-time insights into the roadmap's progress.

Tools such as project management software, dashboards, and Key Performance Indicators (KPIs) are useful for tracking performance and identifying areas for improvement.

Reporting mechanisms should be transparent and accessible to relevant stakeholders, allowing for clear communication across departments.

Regularly scheduled progress meetings provide a forum for teams to discuss challenges, celebrate successes, and share updates, creating an environment of continuous improvement and alignment.

Create a Timeline with Quarterly Goals

Breaking down the roadmap into quarterly goals enables teams to focus on immediate priorities while keeping an eye on long-term objectives.

Set specific goals for each quarter, ensuring that they contribute to the broader vision.

This approach allows teams to concentrate on short-term achievements that build momentum and keep the organization on track to meet year-end targets.

Quarterly goals provide opportunities to evaluate progress, make adjustments, and realign efforts as needed.

This flexibility ensures that the organization remains adaptable to changing conditions and can pivot quickly if market conditions shift or new opportunities arise.

Plan for Flexibility and Adaptability

While a strategic roadmap provides structure, it's important to remain flexible.

Unexpected challenges or opportunities may require adjustments to the plan, and leaders should be prepared to adapt.

Regularly review and adjust the roadmap based on feedback, performance data, and emerging trends to keep the organization agile and responsive.

Flexibility is especially crucial in today's dynamic business environment, where market shifts and technological advancements can impact priorities.

By building adaptability into the roadmap, organizations can respond effectively to change without losing sight of their core goals.

Communicate the Roadmap to the Organization

Once the roadmap is set up, communicate it clearly to the entire organization. Ensure that every team member understands the vision, goals, and milestones and knows how their role contributes to the larger strategy.

Clear communication fosters alignment, engagement, and commitment across departments, creating a shared sense of purpose.

Regular updates and feedback sessions help maintain momentum and keep everyone informed of progress and adjustments.

By creating a transparent, collaborative approach, leaders ensure that the roadmap becomes a living, evolving document that guides the organization's journey toward growth and innovation.

Creating a strategic roadmap for the new year involves more than just setting goals — it requires a thoughtful, structured approach that empowers teams, aligns resources, and supports continuous growth.

By following these steps, organizations can create a roadmap that is both ambitious and achievable, setting the stage for a successful year ahead.

Practical Tools: the New Year Roadmap Template, Quarterly Goals, and Action Plans

Creating a strategic roadmap requires practical tools that help translate vision into actionable steps.

Here, we introduce several tools — including a new year roadmap template, quarterly goal-setting framework, and action plan checklist — that can guide your organization's journey through the coming year.

These tools provide structure and clarity, making it easier for teams to stay aligned and achieve objectives.

the New Year Roadmap Template

A roadmap template serves as a high-level blueprint for the year, outlining key initiatives, goals, and milestones across departments. This template is typically visual, allowing stakeholders to see progress at a glance.

Here's a breakdown of a new year roadmap template:

1. **Vision Statement:** Include a brief statement of the organization's vision for the year, clarifying long-term aspirations.
2. **Strategic Goals:** List 3-5 key goals that align with the organization's mission, such as improving customer

satisfaction, increasing market share, or enhancing sustainability efforts.

3. **Quarterly Breakdown:** Divide the roadmap into quarters, specifying main initiatives for each period. Each quarter should build toward the year-end objectives.
4. **Milestones and Deadlines:** Define major milestones and deadlines for each initiative, helping teams stay on track.
5. **Metrics and KPIs:** Identify metrics to measure progress and success. These KPIs provide a tangible way to assess performance throughout the year.
6. **Ownership and Accountability:** Assign each goal or milestone to a team or individual, clarifying responsibilities and fostering accountability.

This roadmap template serves as a guiding document, providing an overarching view of the year's priorities and allowing teams to visualize how each quarter contributes to the organization's success.

Quarterly Goals Framework

Setting quarterly goals breaks down the roadmap into manageable sections, ensuring focus and momentum. Here's a framework for defining quarterly goals:

1. **Identify Priority Goals:** Select the most critical goals for each quarter, ensuring they align with annual objectives.
2. **Set SMART Goals:** Use the SMART criteria to ensure each goal is clear, achievable, and time-bound.
3. **Define Key Actions:** List 3-5 specific actions required to achieve each goal, such as launching a product, hosting a workshop, or conducting a market analysis.

4. **Set a Timeline for Completion:** Establish deadlines for each action step, making it easier to track progress and stay on schedule.
5. **Monitor Progress with Checkpoints:** Schedule checkpoints throughout the quarter to review progress, address obstacles, and make necessary adjustments.

This quarterly framework encourages consistent progress, making it easier to track achievements, address challenges, and pivot when needed.

Action Plan Checklist

An action plan checklist provides a detailed view of the steps needed to accomplish specific goals or projects.

Use the following checklist as a guide to creating an action plan that supports your new year roadmap:

1. **Goal Definition:** Clearly define the goal and how it aligns with the organization's strategy.
2. **Key Milestones:** Identify key milestones that mark significant progress toward the goal.
3. **Action Steps:** Outline each step required to reach the goal, including tasks, resources, and support needed.
4. **Assign Roles:** Specify who is responsible for each action step, ensuring accountability.
5. **Set Deadlines:** Assign realistic deadlines for each step, keeping the timeline aligned with quarterly goals.
6. **Resources Required:** List resources, such as budget, personnel, and tools, needed to accomplish each step.
7. **Risk Assessment:** Identify potential risks and challenges, as well as contingency plans to address them.

8. **Performance Metrics:** Establish metrics to evaluate success and make data-driven decisions.
9. **Feedback and Adjustments:** Incorporate regular feedback loops, allowing for adjustments as the project progresses.

This checklist keeps projects organized and accountable, ensuring that each action step directly supports quarterly and annual objectives.

Dashboard for Progress Tracking

A dashboard provides a centralized view of the roadmap, enabling teams to track progress, review metrics, and stay aligned.

Use digital tools like Trello, Asana, or a custom Excel sheet to build a dashboard that includes:

1. **Real-Time Metrics:** Track KPIs in real-time, allowing teams to assess progress and make adjustments as needed.
2. **Project Status Updates:** Display the current status of each project or milestone, including whether it's on track, delayed, or completed.
3. **Resource Allocation Overview:** Monitor resource usage to ensure initiatives are supported adequately.
4. **Team Member Contributions:** Include sections that display who is responsible for each task, fostering accountability and transparency.

A well-organized dashboard provides a holistic view of the roadmap, making it easier for leaders and team members to stay informed, motivated, and proactive.

Monthly Review and Adjustment Meetings

Regular check-ins allow teams to review progress, celebrate achievements, and identify areas for improvement.

Host monthly review meetings to:

1. **Assess Goal Progress:** Review each team's progress toward their quarterly goals and address any delays.
2. **Identify Challenges:** Discuss any obstacles and brainstorm solutions as a group.
3. **Make Adjustments:** Adjust the roadmap or action plan based on feedback, ensuring flexibility.
4. **Celebrate Successes:** Recognize accomplishments to keep teams motivated and engaged.

Monthly reviews keep the roadmap dynamic and responsive, ensuring the organization remains adaptable to changing needs and conditions.

By using these practical tools, organizations can create a new year roadmap that is actionable, transparent, and aligned with strategic priorities.

These tools transform ambitious goals into a structured plan, equipping teams to approach the new year with clarity, purpose, and readiness to achieve meaningful results.

Chapter 9: Committing to Growth and Innovation in the New Year

As we reach the end of this journey through essential strategies for the new year and beyond, it's clear that growth and innovation are not just goals but commitments.

Navigating today's complex landscape requires dedication, adaptability, and a vision that aligns with core values.

The insights in this guide have highlighted the importance of purpose-driven innovation, strategic planning, sustainable practices, and creating a roadmap that fosters resilience.

Each chapter has provided tools and strategies designed to empower organizations to embrace change, seize opportunities, and face challenges with confidence.

However, the path to growth is continuous, and every journey begins with a first step. In the coming year, take these insights from planning to action, empowering your teams to contribute, innovate, and thrive.

At Origami Group, we're dedicated to supporting you every step of the way.

Whether you're taking the initial steps toward innovation or refining an existing strategy, our team is here to guide you, providing the expertise and resources needed to help you realize your vision.

Together, let's make the new year coming defined by purposeful progress, sustainable growth, and lasting impact.

Encouragement to Take the First Steps Toward Implementing These Insights

Starting the journey toward innovation and growth can feel overwhelming, especially when facing the rapid changes and complexities of today's business world.

However, the journey toward purposeful growth doesn't have to be daunting; it can be broken down into achievable steps that bring your vision to life one initiative at a time.

As you prepare for the new year, remember that the first step, no matter how small, is the most important. Each action you take sets your organization in motion, building momentum that drives progress, resilience, and ultimately, lasting success.

Begin with a Clear and Purpose-Driven Vision

Your organization's vision is the foundation of every initiative, project, and decision you'll make.

This vision should be inspiring yet attainable, guiding your team's efforts and aligning their contributions with the broader mission.

Take the time to articulate a vision that resonates with everyone in your organization, from leadership to the newest employees.

Make this vision visible in your workspace, incorporate it into meetings, and communicate it regularly.

When everyone shares a common goal, it creates a sense of unity and purpose, motivating each team member to contribute meaningfully to the organization's growth.

Identify Immediate Priorities and Take Action

With a clear vision in place, identify a few immediate priorities that align with your long-term objectives.

Start by focusing on high-impact areas that can yield tangible results, such as customer experience, product development, or sustainability initiatives.

By narrowing your focus, you make it easier to mobilize resources and measure progress. As you tackle these priorities, celebrate small victories and keep teams engaged by recognizing their efforts.

Taking action on even a single initiative demonstrates your commitment to growth and inspires confidence in the journey ahead.

Empower Teams to Innovate and Contribute

Encourage your teams to take ownership of their roles and innovate within their areas of responsibility.

Create an environment where ideas can flow freely, and team members feel comfortable experimenting, even if that means learning from mistakes.

Empowered teams are more likely to take initiative, share creative solutions, and collaborate to achieve shared goals.

Provide resources, training, and support that allow them to develop their skills, enhance their knowledge, and contribute to the organization's success.

Innovation doesn't always have to come from the top; often, the most valuable insights and solutions come from those closest to the work.

Establish a Roadmap and Set Quarterly Goals

A strategic roadmap helps turn your vision into actionable steps. Develop a roadmap that includes specific goals for each quarter, breaking down the journey into manageable phases.

Quarterly goals provide structure and a clear timeline, ensuring that progress is steady and continuous.

They also allow for flexibility, enabling you to make adjustments as you learn from each milestone.

Make this roadmap accessible to all team members, keeping everyone aligned and focused on the tasks at hand.

Regularly revisit the roadmap to assess progress, celebrate achievements, and refine goals as needed.

Cultivate a Culture of Learning and Adaptability

A growth-focused organization is one that embraces learning and is prepared to adapt. Encourage your teams to view challenges as opportunities for growth, fostering a culture where continuous improvement is valued.

Offer opportunities for training, skill development, and mentorship to empower employees to grow in their roles.

Leaders can model this mindset by remaining open to new ideas, listening to feedback, and staying flexible in the face of change.

A culture that prioritizes learning and adaptability equips the organization to navigate uncertainty with resilience and optimism.

Focus on Sustainability as a Core Strategy

As the world shifts toward sustainability, embedding it into your strategy is more than a trend; it's a responsible approach to growth.

Identify areas where sustainable practices can enhance operations, reduce costs, or create a competitive advantage. Whether it's reducing waste in production, sourcing eco-friendly materials, or implementing energy-efficient processes, sustainable initiatives have a dual impact: they contribute to the organization's growth while making a positive difference in the world.

In the new year, let sustainability be a guiding principle that aligns with your organization's core values and mission.

Leverage Data to Drive Decision-Making

Data is a valuable asset that can guide decision-making, track progress, and refine strategies. Utilize data analytics to measure the effectiveness of your initiatives, identify trends, and understand customer needs.

Data-driven insights allow you to make informed decisions that enhance efficiency, target key areas, and drive innovation.

Establish clear metrics and KPIs for each goal, regularly reviewing them to assess performance and make adjustments as needed.

By incorporating data into your strategy, you ensure that each step forward is backed by evidence and insights.

Build and Nurture Relationships with Stakeholders

Strong relationships with stakeholders—whether they're customers, partners, or employees—are crucial to long-term success.

Communicate your vision, values, and goals transparently, fostering trust and alignment with your stakeholders.

Regularly engage with customers to understand their evolving needs, collaborate with partners who share your values, and maintain open communication with your teams.

By building these relationships, you create a support network that fuels growth, attracts loyalty, and reinforces your organization's mission.

Commit to Continuous Reflection and Improvement

Growth is an ongoing process that requires regular reflection and refinement.

Take time each quarter to evaluate your progress, recognize achievements, and identify areas for improvement.

Encourage teams to share their feedback, celebrate their successes, and learn from any setbacks.

This iterative approach allows you to stay agile, responsive, and focused on your goals.

By consistently reflecting and improving, you ensure that your organization remains resilient, adaptable, and prepared to face the challenges of the new year and beyond.

Take the First Step Today

The journey toward growth and innovation begins with a single step.

It's easy to feel that you need all the answers before taking action, but momentum is built through progress, not perfection.

Start small if necessary, but start with purpose and commitment. Each initiative, no matter how small, contributes to the larger vision and brings your organization closer to its goals.

Taking the first step sends a powerful message to your team and stakeholders: that you are committed to creating a future defined by growth, innovation, and positive impact.

Taking the first steps toward implementing these insights in the new year sets the stage for lasting progress.

Remember, growth is not achieved overnight; it's a series of intentional actions taken consistently over time.

By following these steps, fostering a culture of innovation, and staying committed to your vision, you can lead your organization through a year of purposeful, impactful growth.

Origami Group's Commitment to Supporting Clients on Their Journey

At Origami Group, we believe that every organization has the potential to grow, innovate, and make a positive impact.

Our commitment is to support our clients on this journey by providing the tools, insights, and guidance needed to turn ambitious goals into achievable realities.

As your partner in growth, we understand the challenges you face and are dedicated to helping you navigate them with confidence and purpose.

A Client-Centered Approach to Support

Origami Group's approach begins with understanding each client's unique vision, challenges, and objectives.

We know that no two organizations are alike, which is why we tailor our support to meet the specific needs of each client.

Our team takes the time to listen, learn, and assess where you are on your growth journey, developing customized strategies that align with your mission.

Whether you're a startup seeking to establish a foothold or a well-established organization aiming to adapt to new trends, we're here to help you achieve your goals.

Expertise Across a Range of Industries

With years of experience working across various industries, Origami Group brings a wealth of expertise to every client relationship.

Our team is skilled in areas such as innovation engineering, strategic planning, sustainability, and business development, enabling us to provide comprehensive support that addresses multiple facets of your organization.

This diverse expertise allows us to deliver solutions that are not only innovative but also practical and aligned with industry-specific challenges.

Guidance on Purpose-Driven Innovation

Purpose-driven innovation is a cornerstone of our work at Origami Group. We're dedicated to helping clients develop strategies that align with their core values, ensuring that growth is meaningful and sustainable.

From helping you define a purpose that resonates with stakeholders to implementing practices that reinforce this commitment, we work alongside you to embed purpose into every aspect of your innovation efforts.

Purpose-driven innovation strengthens brand identity, builds customer loyalty, and fosters long-term resilience, and we're here to guide you through each step of this transformative journey.

Customized Roadmap Development and Strategic Planning

A well-structured roadmap is essential for turning vision into action. Our team assists clients in creating detailed, actionable roadmaps that guide them through the year and beyond.

By working with you to define objectives, set milestones, and establish clear metrics, we ensure that your strategic plan is both ambitious and achievable.

With our support, you can focus on immediate priorities while keeping an eye on long-term goals, ensuring that each step you take brings you closer to sustainable growth.

Support in Implementing Sustainable Practices

At Origami Group, we recognize the importance of sustainability in today's business landscape. We offer guidance on implementing sustainable practices that enhance efficiency, reduce environmental impact, and align with consumer expectations.

From eco-friendly product design to responsible supply chain management, we provide the insights and tools needed to make sustainability an integral part of your business strategy.

By adopting sustainable practices, our clients not only contribute to a healthier planet but also strengthen their brand reputation and appeal to environmentally conscious customers.

Continuous Support and Adaptability

Change is a constant in the business world, and staying agile is essential for success.

Origami Group is committed to providing continuous support, ensuring that our clients remain adaptable and responsive to new challenges and opportunities.

Through regular check-ins, progress reviews, and adjustment sessions, we work with you to refine strategies, make informed decisions, and address any emerging issues.

Our adaptive approach allows us to support your organization's growth journey in real time, helping you pivot when needed and stay on course for success.

Access to Practical Tools and Resources

We equip our clients with practical tools and resources that make implementing growth strategies easier and more effective.

From customizable roadmap templates to data analysis tools and performance-tracking dashboards, Origami Group provides the resources needed to track progress, manage projects, and measure success.

Our goal is to empower clients to make data-driven decisions, optimize operations, and create a culture of continuous improvement.

Cultivating a Culture of Innovation and Learning

Innovation is at the heart of growth, and Origami Group is dedicated to fostering a culture of creativity and continuous learning within client organizations.

We offer workshops, training programs, and team-building exercises designed to enhance skills, promote collaboration, and encourage innovative thinking.

By nurturing a culture where curiosity and adaptability are valued, we help clients create an environment where teams feel empowered to contribute ideas, experiment, and innovate.

Celebrating Success and Learning from Challenges

Origami Group believes in celebrating each milestone and learning from every challenge.

As we support clients in reaching their goals, we take time to recognize achievements and assess lessons learned along the way.

This reflective approach enables us to build on successes, address any obstacles, and refine strategies as needed.

By creating a culture of celebration and learning, we help clients stay motivated, resilient, and committed to their journey of growth and innovation.

A Long-Term Partnership Committed to Your Success

At Origami Group, we view our relationship with clients as a long-term partnership.

We are fully committed to supporting your success, not just for one project or year, but for the journey ahead.

Our team is here to provide ongoing guidance, adapt to your evolving needs, and celebrate your achievements as you continue to grow.

Together, we can build a future defined by purposeful innovation, sustainable growth, and positive impact.

Origami Group's commitment to supporting clients on their journey goes beyond providing solutions; it's about empowering organizations to reach their full potential and make a meaningful difference.

As you embark on the new year and beyond, know that Origami Group is here to help you succeed, one step at a time.